The Rich Nations and the Poor Nations

Books by Barbara Ward

THE WEST AT BAY

POLICY FOR THE WEST

FAITH AND FREEDOM

THE INTERPLAY OF EAST AND WEST

FIVE IDEAS THAT CHANGE THE WORLD

INDIA AND THE WEST

THE RICH NATIONS AND THE POOR NATIONS

BARBARA WARD

The Rich Nations
AND
The Poor Nations

W · W · NORTON & COMPANY · INC · New York

TO
J. H. E.

Acknowledgment

The lectures upon which this book is based were
first given for the Canadian Broadcasting Corporation, and are published with their kind permis-
sion. The collection of much of the material used
in the broadcasts was made possible by a generous grant from the Carnegie Foundation.

Contents

The Rich Nations   13

The Poor Nations   37

Communism's Blue Print   62

The Economics of Development   86

The Politics of Development   111

Not by Bread Alone   137

The Rich Nations and the Poor Nations

Chapter One

The Rich Nations

I SUPPOSE we are all aware of the fact that we live in the most catastrophically revolutionary age that men have ever faced. Usually one thinks of a revolution as one event or at least as one interconnected series of events. But we are in fact living with ten or twenty such revolutions—all changing our ways of life, our ways of looking at things, changing everything out of recognition and changing it fast.

What I want to do here is to trace some of these revolutions in their effect on our environment and on the way we live. And since I cannot deal with all of them, I have chosen four which seem to me to weave their way in and out of our lives at every point.

Now, the first and perhaps the most pervasive of these revolutions begins in the field of ideas. This is hardly surprising since ideas are the prime movers of history. Revolutions usually begin with ideas and it is by our ideas that we change the way we live, the way we organize society, the way we manipulate material things. So let us begin with a revolutionary idea now at work from one end of the world to the other: the revolution of equality—equality of men and equality of nations. This is a bald statement. It cannot be treated exhaustively. There is simply not time to explore all the implications of man's equality with man. For one thing, no society yet knows fully what it means by such equality. Is it to be only a levelling? Does it imply indifference to excellence? Can it be combined with reasonable lines of command and control? And, since someone must rule, if all supposedly extraneous obstacles to equality were removed—birth, land, wealth, inheritance—would rule by brain and ability alone create a 'meritocracy,' a 'Mandarinate' of refined intelligence, finally more unequal than a system demanding less rigorous and inflexible methods of recruiting the governing group? These are all fascinating questions to pursue and many of them are strictly relevant to the great international questions of our day. For instance, the recruitment of leaders among the dispossessed in the name of equality is a great strength for Communism, since in all developing nations the dispossessed make up the vast majority. But there must be limits set to our discussion and here we are concerned primarily with equality as a force making for social, economic, and national change.

We know that men's passionate desire to see themselves as the equals of other human beings without distinctions of class or sex or race or nationhood is one of the driving forces of our day. And I believe it is a tap root of modern nationalism. I do not, of course, minimize the other roots of nationalism: the sense of community, the common tongue, the shared history. But when nations look out on the international arena, much of the strength of their nationalism comes from the sense that they are as good as their neighbours and ought to have the same rights; in other words, equality. The whole United Nations with its 'one state, one vote,' reflects this egalitarian nationalism and 'the right to self-determination,' the most cutting edge of nationalism as old empires dissolve, is in essence the new peoples' claim to national equality with the older states. For this reason, nationalism today comes to us in great measure in the form of equality—the equality of nations one with each other, the equality of esteem and prestige which comes from not being run by other nations. This is one of the great drives of our world. And when we discuss nationalism, I think it is legitimate to unite it with the idea of equality.

The second revolution also concerns ideas: the idea of progress, of the possibility of material change leading to a better world, not hereafter, but here and now. This worldliness, if you like, this emphasis on the goods

(15)

and opportunities of this world, is another radical force at work in our world.

The third revolution is a biological revolution: the sudden vast increase in the rate at which the human race is multiplying upon the face of the earth.

The fourth and perhaps the most pervasive of all the revolutions of our day is the application of science and saving—or capital—to all the economic processes of our life. In fact, the application is much wider. We have begun to apply science and reason to nearly all our forms of living, to administration, to office management, to politics, to sociology, even to culture and to art.

These four revolutions—of equality, of this-worldliness, of rising birth-rates, and of driving scientific change—all started in the North Atlantic arena, in those nations which lie around the North Atlantic Ocean. Britain, Western Europe, and North America have, by working and expanding together, created a quite new kind of human society. A sort of mutation has occurred and we in the Atlantic area no longer share a continuous way of life with under-developed and emerging peoples, because in their societies none of the revolutions has been fully at work. They have had little idea of equality. There was in the past no great urge for general material progress. The pressure of population followed a strict rotation of famine and feast and had little of the explosive burst that we have seen in our day. Above all, traditional societies did very little saving and had virtually no science. By the same token, these changes which cut us off from all earlier forms of social organization have created in the Atlantic world what can only be called a new kind of human community.

I do not know whether one would say of this new society that it is demonstrably happier. Sometimes I think people wonder whether it can be said to be more civilized. But there is one thing which is absolutely certain. It is sensationally richer. What has happened around the North Atlantic is that a ring of societies has come into being with more wealth, more economic resources at its disposal, than has ever before been known in human history. This is the profoundly revolutionary change to which all the subsidiary revolutions have contributed. And, since all nations have not yet come within the scope of this revolution, or rather this series of revolutions, and since all of them without exception desire to do so, the distinction between rich nations and poor nations is one of the great dominant political and international themes of our century.

How have these four revolutions, working together, produced the mutation of a quite new kind of society: the wealthy or affluent society? How is it that, remoulding the traditional forms of social order, they have developed a form of society so different from any that went before? Let us begin with the revolution of equality. It has its roots in two profound traditions of Western society: the Greek view of law and the Judeo-Christian vision of souls all equal in the sight of God. For the Greek, the essence of citizenship, what distinguished the *polis*—the city-state—from the barbarians outside, was that men lived in the Greek city according to laws which they themselves had helped to frame. This was not a full vision of equality; slaves and women were excluded. But the citizen enjoyed equality with his fellows before the law and the law was the final shield of his integrity and equality against the threat of tyranny; either the tyranny of a single leader or the possibly more dangerous threat of an arbitrary majority. Here in its first emergence in history could be found a definition of the 'rights of man' in terms of his rights against a dangerously sovereign government.

The other mood of equality is expressed in Christian metaphysics, in the vision of souls standing equal in the sight of God. During the Middle Ages, cathedral and church were the educators of the common man and a favourite theme in those days was the 'Doom,' or Last Judgment, carved above the portals of cathedrals or painted on the humbler walls of parish churches. From these panoramas of bliss and misery men received with vivid emotional force the sense of human equality. Among those called to bliss would be the shepherd, the peasant, the woodman, the carpenter, while those descending with tortured faces to everlasting misery were all too often kings, princes, dukes, and bishops as well. Here, expressed with the most dramatic sense of contrast, is the profound root of equality: the belief that souls are equal before God and that, therefore, their equality is innate, metaphysical, and independent of the vanities of class, race, or culture. Clearly, once you implant an idea as revolutionary as this in the soil of society, you can have no conception of the luxuriance and diversity of the growth that may follow. And one consequence in our Western civilization is especially worth examining. It is the emergence to a dominant position in society of men and groups who have never achieved a political 'break-through' in any other civilization.

Since the beginning of history, you can say in shorthand that the dominant rulers have been the kings and the priests. They were flanked by the warriors, and often, as in the early Middle Ages in Europe, warriors were rewarded for their services with fiefs of land. Or, as in India, land revenue was allotted to court officials and advisers as a source of income. Thus the political leadership of the community came to be monopolized by the court and by landed men. In such societies—and most traditional societies resemble this pattern—the merchant was of necessity a marginal figure. To this day, in parts of Latin America and Asia, this old, more or less feudal pattern persists. But as the Middle Ages unfolded in Europe a different picture began to appear. Owing to the division of power between Pope and Emperor at the head of society, the possibility of a plurality of powers opened up for the whole social order. Subsidiary groups—nations, cities, communes, corporations—grasped the power needed for their operations, defined it in terms of law, and defended it in the name of equal rights. In such a society the merchant was able to exercise real power and to enjoy real security for his work, his trade, and his savings. The charters given to cities defined his rights of self-government and, as early as the fourteenth century, the sovereign called him into consultation—through parliament—before trying to tax his wealth for national purposes.

These developments gave the cities with their merchants and bankers and rising middle classes an independence they enjoyed nowhere else. There was never any figure in Delhi or Canton who had the status, influence, and rights, of the Lord Mayor of London or the Burgomaster of Ghent. And without the self-confidence and security of the merchant class the later evolution of capitalist society would have been inconceivable.

But of course the leaven of equality did not cease to operate once it had raised the middle classes to effective influence. It worked right on through the rest of society and it works on to this day. In England's Civil War it was John Lilburne, a soldier on the more extreme wing in Cromwell's Army, who gave classic expression to the drive which would dominate politics for the next four hundred years. 'The poorest he that is in England has a life to live as the richest he.' This was Lilburne's phrase and ever since it has been the motive power of revolutions beyond number. It underlies the growth of socialism, the cutting edge of trade union organization, the emancipation of the workers in the wake of the middle classes, the whole concept of the modern welfare state. We do not see the end of the process for, as I suggested earlier, we do not know what the ultimate stage of equality may be. Is it level equalness? Is it equal chance and opportunity? Is it conceivably a society ruled by love, not force?

We do not know. But we *do* know that the leaven of equality has worked through every stratum of our society, emancipating new classes and letting loose new political forces onto the great stage of history. Now we have to ask the question: What in the main have these new classes asked for in claiming their emancipation? At this point we meet the second of our revolutionary ideas: the idea of what one might call this-worldliness, of immense interest in *this* world, in its processes, in its laws and construction, in the ways in which it can be set to work and made over according to human ends and purposes—in a word, the world as an arena of work and effort where needs and dreams can be satisfied.

These ideas spring essentially from our triple inheritance: Greek thought, Judaism, and Christianity. It was in the Greek vision of law that science acquired its fundamental confidence in a material universe predictable and orderly enough to be explored. From the Judeo-Christian religious inheritance came the idea that the whole of creation is God's work, and as such must be of immense interest and value. 'Call thou no thing unclean' was the divine instruction to Peter and, in spite of the temptations of religious pessimism, Christianity has never dismissed as 'illusion' what comes from the hand of God. Other societies have lacked this essential insight into the value of created things. In Hindu culture, for instance, the world is *Maya*, illusion, a fevered dance of fleeting appearances which mask the pure reality of uncreated being.

But perhaps the sharpest break in Western tradition from the basic ideas of other civilizations lies in its vision of reality as an unfolding drama, as an immense dialogue between God and man crowned at some inconceivable end in an outcome of fulfilment and bliss. All archaic societies feel themselves bound to a 'melancholy wheel' of endless recurrence. Seasons, the life cycle, planetary order, all revealed the return of things to their origins, and life swung round in the orbit fixed by destiny. Marcus Aurelius, wisest of Roman emperors, believed that at forty a man had experienced all there was to experience. No vision of reality as progressing forward to new possibilities, no sense of the future as better and fuller than the present, tempered the underlying fatalism of ancient civilization. It is only in the Jewish and Christian faith that a Messianic hope first breaks upon mankind. In Christianity, the hope is expressed in religious terms of deliverance and salvation. But over the centuries the idea became transmuted into this-worldly terms, in fact into the dominant idea of progress, of getting forward, of being able to see hope ahead, and of working for a better future, not hereafter, but here and now.

Now let us examine the effect of this respect for material things, coupled with a Messianic hope of the future, upon one aspect of Western society—upon its economic system. As the Middle Ages ended and the merchants felt their status and their opportunities increase, they found in the Christian tradition those elements which best suited their outlook and condition.

Opposing the luxuries of the courts and the loudly alleged idleness of monastic living, they preached a gospel of work, praising the religious value of what men did in the counting house, in the workshop, in farm and field, and looking forward to the coming of the Kingdom in terms of work, effort, and material success. No one can doubt that, as a result, an immense charge of energy was added to the urge to work and produce at the beginning of the capitalist era.

But there were still limits to the merchant's materialism. As workers, they stood out against an idle and luxurious world. To acquire wealth was one thing; to spend it in riotous living quite another. So, instead, they accumulated capital and set it working further. This restraint was one of the roots of saving on a large scale without which sufficient capital might never have been accumulated for the modern economic system. Work, austerity, and an increasingly secularized version of the Messianic hope were thus the ferments of a new society, the portents of a revolutionary age when the desire for better things and 'the revolution of rising expectations'—to use Mr. Adlai Stevenson's phrase—would engulf the whole world.

Before we leave these mutations in the Western idea, we should also examine the extent to which equality and material progress have enlarged the concept of the nation. Undoubtedly today the main drives behind the idea of nationhood, especially in the emergent territories, are equality and material progress. Nevertheless nationalism as such is so deeply rooted in human affairs that we must make a brief detour to examine it in its own terms. It begins with the tribe. The tribe is the oldest of human associations, a total community bound by links of kinship and blood, all too often propelled into action by the sense of having competing interests with other tribes, which it fights for hunting fields and grazing areas and, when conflict becomes insoluble, involves in tragic wars of extermination.

In large parts of Africa, this original organization of mankind remains and, as the collapse of the Congo has shown, easily reverts to violence and destruction. But in other continents wider forms of political organization have developed. We move on from the tribe to congeries of tribes and to the union of different tribes under conquering dynasties or empires. In these wider states the sense of blood kinship is lessened. Wars of imperial conquest take the place of wars of tribal extermination. Professional armies arise in place of a people armed *en masse*. In large parts of Asia and for long years under the Roman Empire in Europe, wars changed the leadership of the state and the distribution of power, but the life of the peasants and villages and country towns continued with relatively little disturbance. Throughout northern India, for instance, after the collapse of organized imperial rule, Rajput princes fought each other continuously while the villagers took virtually no part in the wars.

This relative discontinuity between rulers and ruled began to end when, towards the end of the Middle Ages, a new sense of blood brotherhood and cohesion

was restored to the political community in Western
Europe. At that time Europe began to reacquire an
almost tribal sense of the state. It had been dynastic.
The Plantagenets, the Capets, were symbols and leaders
of their peoples but, owing to the coincidence of language and frontiers in Western Europe, people began
to discover again a sense of kinship based upon what
they came to feel was almost common blood, an organic
family unity. So the nation-state has in it some element
of the tribe, operating at a more elaborate and a more
organized level.

Now this almost tribal concept of the nation had
extremely important effects both in the development
of the modern economy and in the development of the
West's relations with the rest of the world. Modern
capitalist society needs a certain scale of market if it
is to gain anything from the division of labour and the
diversification of work and product. The nation-state
provided a framework cohesive enough to act as an enlarged market. Merchants felt that they had a common
unit in which to work. They moved on from the highly
restricted market of the village, the estate, or the river
valley to the larger market of the nation. And they
moved on with all the more vigour and all the more
drive because they were competing with other nations
who were developing their own markets in the same
sense: British merchants competing with French merchants, French with Dutch, Dutch with Portuguese,
and so forth. The nation defined the market and then,
reciprocally, the interests of the market helped to under-

line the exclusiveness of nationhood.

The effect was not limited to Western Europe. Out of the intense rivalry came the great thrust which led to the colonial control of most of the world by these same Western nations. Arabs, after all, had been out trading in Asia for generations before the Westerners arrived. But the trade was peaceful and did not impinge much on local politics. What the Westerners brought with them was a fierce competitive determination to cut other nations off from the profits of the new oriental trade. This led to the struggle for the control of the seas. And, if one follows the process closely in such areas as Indonesia or India, one can see how the determination of the Dutch to throw everybody else out, or the determination of the British not to allow the French to maintain a foothold, afterwards led to the kind of jockeying and maneuvering and backing of local rulers that, little by little, brought about the extension of Western colonial control to the whole area.

At this point it should be easier to understand why modern nationalism has such deep roots in the ideas of equality and material progress. The Western traders-turned-rulers in Asia took their fierce exclusive nationalism into societies still loosely united as dynastic or imperial states. There they settled down to make money, to trade, to build up export industries, and to set in motion some of the economic processes which underpin the modern economy. They carried with them a concern for progress, for material well-being, for this-worldliness, all unknown in Eastern lands. They began to spur local peoples to think in this same sense.

At the same time, they created a nationalist reaction against their own nationalist pretensions. By ruling other groups in the name of their own national interests, they taught these groups to see themselves as nations and to claim equality for their own rights. There was no 'nationalism' in India until Britain aroused it by teaching Indians the ideals of nationhood and at the same time denying them the rights of national self-determination. Material progress and equality have been the great spurs to nationalism throughout the colonial world, and the reason is simply that it was in the mood of national self-assertion and economic advantage that Westerners established and maintained their rule.

Now let us turn to the third of the revolutions that have created the metamorphosis of Western society. From the eighteenth century onwards new medical sciences and steady advances in public sanitation, coupled with the crowding of more and more people into the new cities, lengthened life and set in process an explosion of the birth-rate. In the West, on the whole, this explosion has proved a boost to growth, a boost to wealth, a boost to economic development. The reason is, in the main, that the creation and expansion of the modern economic system came into being while the explosion of population was still in its early stages. In fact, as population grew the economy could grow with it. There was a time in the eighteenth century when it looked as though a shortage of manpower would set a definite limit to the growth of economy. In nineteenth-century America massive immigration was one of the great spurs to economic growth. In the nineteen-twenties and -thirties, the Depression coincided, earlier in Britain and later in America, with a considerable falling off in the birth-rate. Today, once again, it seems certain that some aspects of American growth are greatly stimulated by its spurt in population. So, on the whole, economic growth and growth in population have gone together in the West. That they have not done so in the East is one of the world's great problems. But in the West the dilemma of population outstripping resources has not occurred. On the contrary, an expanding manpower, absorbed into an expanding economic system, has provided labour for the production of goods and a consumers' market for their sale.

Now we come to the last of our revolutions, the most pervasive of all, that of capital and science, and the application of both to our economic processes.

Now, capital is saving; and saving means not consuming. But there is no point in delaying or cutting back consumption unless, at some point, the saving made will result in more consumption later on. For example, it takes more effort, time, and input to produce a better seed or to develop a better plough. But in the end you are rewarded with a better harvest; in other words, consumption can go up as a result of the extra effort.

The trouble with traditional society is quite simply this: man's knowledge of how material things behave is still very limited. He has not yet developed the habits and tools of science and experiment to explore all the ways in which matter can be changed and manipulated. There are few ways known of making better seeds; not very much has been tried in the way of constructing better ploughs; better ploughs have to wait on more refined techniques for dealing with iron ore; and experiments with iron ore have in turn to wait on finding a substitute for charcoal. In short, the heat of wood, the energy of wind and water, the speed of a horse, the skill of the hand still represent the outer limits of a very restricted technology.

The great change that occurred in the eighteenth century was above all an enormous expansion in the techniques and technologies to which savings could be devoted. This change came about because of the revolutionary change we have already discussed: the West's steadily increasing interest in material things, in this-worldliness, and in the purposive exploration of physical reality.

We take this attitude so entirely for granted that it is easy to forget how recent it is and how entirely its origins lie in our Western society. The scientific spirit, drawing on the Greek sense of law and the Judeo-Christian respect for the handiwork of God, is perhaps the most profoundly distinguishing feature of our civilization. Science could hardly arise in Hindu society since one does not devote a lifetime to exploring an illusion. It did not arise in China, for in spite of orderly government, rational rule, and intense intellectual interest stretching back through millennia into the past, the dominant Confucian class turned its back on science and preferred instead the consideration of human relations and urbane life.

But in the West, the aftermath of the Wars of Religion was to turn educated opinion to the examination of material things in which, it was hoped, the clash of dogma could be left behind. As a result, in the seventeenth and eighteenth centuries, all over Western Europe, especially in Britain, the inventors and experimenters set to work to explore matter and improve technology. They revolutionized the use of iron. They transformed textile machinery. They invented the steam engine. The age of the railways and the factory system opened up ahead.

An emancipated and self-confident merchant class, with a strongly developed credit system, had savings to pour into these new technologies. They were joined by enlightened gentleman farmers and by sturdy self-reliant artisans, all ready to experiment and back the experiments with their own—and other people's—savings. This combination of new technology and expanded saving made possible great increases in productivity. Much more could be produced by each pair of hands in each working hour. The surplus could be reinvested in further expansion. This process depended on keeping general consumption low. The mass of workers did not at first profit from the new system. Herded into the towns, ignorant, unorganized, they contributed the massive new saving by working for wages which were much lower than their true productivity. But the savings were made by entrepreneurs who reinvested them to expand the whole scale of the economy.

Out of this massive 'primitive accumulation' came what one might call a 'break-through' to a new type of economy where, with fresh capital applied to all the processes of production, the expansion of each helped the expansion of all with a sort of internal momentum which finally put the economy into orbit as the new type of advanced, capitalized, industrialized, techno-logical society that we see around us in the West today.

These then, are the four revolutions that have trans-formed traditional society to give us the modern world. It is above all in the North Atlantic community that all of them have in fact started, grown, interacted upon each other, and come together to create a quite new kind of society. First, the 'break-through' came in Brit-ain. Then it followed in countries resembling Britain in basic social pre-conditions: the dominance of the merchant class, the relative openness of society, the pressure upwards of new social groups—merchants, workers, and farmers—and the basic attitudes of scientific interest and material ambition. Especially in empty lands settled by Europeans overseas, and above all in the United States, there occurred a mutual flow of capital, a mutual interdependence of trade which meant that all these lands helped to draw each other up the spiral of expanding production: Britain sparking growth in Europe; British and European investment spurring expansion in the United States. As early as the 1870s, the North Atlantic countries were providing over sixty per cent of the foreign capital loaned in these areas and were together engrossing something like seventy per cent of world trade.

The degree to which this interdependence stimulated the expansion of new wealth can, I think, be shown perhaps better by our failures than by our successes. This Atlantic society can still be wealthier than any known to man, in spite of the fact that it has contrived in the seventy to a hundred years of its interdependence to fight two wars of such appalling, such drastic, such monstrous destruction that one might have conceived that no people on earth could have recovered their wealth after such an outpouring of waste and carnage. But no; this interdependent community, even interdependent when fighting within itself, has been able to drag itself out of these holocausts and to achieve levels of wealth and well-being even greater than anything that went before. This, I think, is the most startling measure of the effectiveness of the new methods of science, the new methods of technology, the whole new field of saving applied to the production of wealth.

Nor is the story finished. On the contrary; at the present moment this group of wealthy countries—Great Britain, the white Dominions of the British Commonwealth, the United States, and Western Europe—represent a capacity, not only for present wealth but for future wealth of which we really have no very clear sense. Changes in technology are becoming more frequent and drastic. New frontiers open up in energy, in chemicals, in ever wider applications of science to production. Above all, we do not produce at full stretch. The scale of our reserves is illustrated by the fact that we only put our productive machine fully to work when, in war, we are all vowed to destruction. Our most productive periods are those in which we are destroying most fully what we make. And from this folly, we are not yet released, owing to the fabulous weight of our armament programs.

So this enormously wealthy community of nations is growing wealthier and could grow wealthier still. But at the same time it is not now having a comparable effect on the rest of the world. In the nineteenth century, a portion of the capital that went out in search of profits from this growing wealthy community did go out to the colonies, to India, to the Far East, to Latin America; and part of the growth of the Atlantic world was in some measure sparked by buying the raw materials of less developed countries overseas. But in the twentieth century, this kind of interdependence between an industrial centre and the producers of raw materials on the fringe has tended to weaken. In the last twenty or thirty years, the West has grown much more rapidly in internal production than it has in its need for imports. We are no longer, in the hopeful nineteenth-century sense, necessarily dragging up the rest of the world in our wake. The automatic stimulus we give to growth overseas is now much less than it was even seventy years ago; and this is because of a very profound change in our industrial processes. We apply science so much more freely through changed technology that the art of the substitute has come to a quite new effectiveness. Very often the imported raw materials on which we used to depend can now be produced within our own frontiers. One thinks of artificial rubber, new fabrics for textiles, petro-chemicals, conceivably even *ersatz* chocolate. And so, we no longer automatically exercise the same pull of development on the outside world as we did in our early days of growth and wealth. We have been filling the gap with extraordinary economic assistance. But we do not look on this 'job' as a settled commitment. It is still a precarious expedient; and in any case it is too small.

Then there is another big change which alters the relationship. It is quite simply that the West has completed its 'break-through' to modernization and the emergent countries have not. Above all, they have not completed the first, hard, even merciless, phase of early saving.

To begin the whole process of saving is a massive task. A sort of momentum has to be achieved. All parts of the economy have to be affected if the economic pattern as a whole is to change. A little modification here, a little development there, may transform parts of the economy, but it is only when the flood of change begins to run right through society that you get that actual 'break-through' to a new type of productive economy which has occurred in the West. But naturally, this 'break-through' occurring in a traditional society, demands an immense amount of capital. You have to begin to modify almost everything; education, farming, transport, power, industry—all have to change. This means that capital is required not in little amounts, but on a massive scale. And yet society, being under-developed, is still too poor for savings on such a scale. This is the paradox of the phase which Marx called 'primitive accumulation'—the first great effort of saving which has to be achieved if the new momentum is to begin. The Western colonial impact on the rest of the world did not create such a momentum. It created partial modernization: the beginnings of modern education and industry, some cash farming directed to export markets, some ports, some transport, some beginnings of modern administration. But all this did not amount to the full momentum of sustained growth.

The result is that the gap between those Western lands that are already 'in orbit' in their economic life, and those that are not yet off the ground, is tending at the moment to grow wider, not narrower. We in the West have long completed our first phase of primitive accumulation; we have a machine in being to use for further expansion; and, incidentally, we contrived to acquire that machine while our population was still at a relatively low level. Now that we are 'in orbit,' our own wealth can multiply by compound interest because we are already wealthy. This, after all, is a cycle we recognize very well in family life. It is very much easier for a rich man to invest and grow richer than for the poor man to begin investing at all. And this is also true of nations. Nations that are not yet through the 'sound barrier' of saving are tending to get poorer with the

CYCLE WE
RECOGNIZE
IN FAMILY
LIFE

added complication that their populations are meanwhile going steadily up.

So our world today is dominated by a complex and tragic division. One part of mankind has undergone the revolutions of modernization and has emerged on the other side to a pattern of great and increasing wealth. But most of the rest of mankind has yet to achieve any of the revolutions; they are caught off balance before the great movement of economic and social momentum can be launched. Their old traditional world is dying. The new radical world is not yet born. This being so, the gap between the rich and the poor has become inevitably the most tragic and urgent problem of our day.

Chapter Two

The Poor Nations

HOW ARE we to define the 'poor' nations? The phrase 'under-developed' is not very satisfactory for it groups together very different types of under-development. India and Pakistan, for instance, are heirs of a great and ancient civilization and have many of the other attributes—in art, literature, and administration—of developed states, even though they are also very poor. Other areas—one thinks of the Congo—are developed in virtually no sense at all. I think, therefore, that perhaps the most satisfactory method of defining poverty at this stage is to discuss the question simply in terms of per-capita income—the average income available to citizens in the various countries. If you fix the level of wealth of 'wealthy' communities at a per-capita income of about $500 a year, then eighty per cent of mankind lives below it. It is chiefly among the privileged nations living round the North Atlantic that we find levels of annual income above the 500-dollar mark. Indeed, in the United States or Canada, it is three and four times above the minimum. Australia and New Zealand also belong to this group. In the Communist bloc, Czechoslovakia is moving up into it, and so is Russia. In fact, it is a marginal question whether they should not now be included among the rich. But what is certain is that the mass of mankind live well below the income level of $500 per head a year; and in some countries—one thinks particularly of India —per-capita income may be as low as $60. Yet between 400 and 500 million people live in India—something like two-fifths of all the poor people in the uncommitted world. So the gap between rich and poor is tremendous and, as we have already noticed, it is tending to widen further.

What is the cause of this? Why is there this great blanket of poverty stretched across the face of the globe? Before we attempt an answer, we should, I think, remember that ours is the first century in which such a question can even be put. Poverty has been the universal lot of man until our own day. No one asked fundamental questions about a state of affairs which everyone took for granted. The idea that the majority could have access to a little modest affluence is wholly new, the break-through of whole communities to national wealth totally unprecedented.

To return to our question: the contrast between the wealth of the West and the poverty of nearly everybody else does have some puzzling features. For centuries, for millennia, the East had been the region of known and admired wealth. It was to the Orient that men looked when they spoke of traditional forms of riches: gold and diamonds, precious ointments, rare spices, extravagant brocades and silks. In fact, for over a thousand years, one of the great drives in the Western economy was to open trade with the wealthier East. And one of the problems facing that trade—as far in the past as in the days of imperial Rome—was the West's inability to provide very much in return. It is hard to sell bear rugs to merchants at Madras, especially during the monsoon. Nor is the contrast between the East's endowment and the relative poverty of the West simply a matter of history. Today, for instance, Indonesia seems obviously better endowed in a whole range of ways than are some European countries—one might perhaps pick Norway.

In spite of these puzzles, there are some underlying physical causes which explain why some countries have been left behind in the world's present thrust towards greater wealth. Many of the tropical soils have been submitted to millennia of leaching under the downpour of heavy rains and are precarious soils for agriculture. Nor is the climate of tropical regions precisely designed for work. When the temperature rises to ninety degrees and the humidity to ninety per cent, you do not feel like rushing out and solving one of the first problems in Euclid. Even less do you want to cut a tree —favourite occupation of Victorian gentlemen—or dig a ditch.

Wherever the monsoon is the rain-bringing force, there is an underlying element of instability in farming. The concentration of rain in a few months creates expensive problems of control and storage. Rivers vary from raging torrents to dry beds. And if the monsoons fail in India or South-east Asia, then there is quite simply no agriculture because there is no water.

Another fact making for poverty is that the great tropical belt stretching round the world has only limited sources of energy: no coal and not too much oil outside the Middle East, Venezuela, and Indonesia. One must conclude, therefore, that certain original differences exist in the actual endowment of resources in the advancing Northern Hemisphere and the relatively stagnant South. Nonetheless, I think the profound reason for the contrast of wealth and poverty lies in the fact that the various revolutions which have swept over the face of the Western world in the last hundred years exist at only a chaotic or embryonic stage among the poorer states.

The biological revolution of more rapid growth in population is on the way in these areas. But the other vast changes—an intellectual revolution of materialism and this-worldliness, the political revolution of equality, and above all the scientific and technological revolution which comes from the application of savings and the sciences to the whole business of daily life—are only beginning the process of transforming every idea and institution in the emergent lands. The revolution of modernization has not yet driven these states into the contemporary world. The greatest drama of our time is that they will be swept onwards. But we are still uncertain over the form these revolutions will finally take. Everywhere they have started; nowhere are they yet complete; but the trend cannot be reversed. The modernizing of the whole world is under way.

Millennia ago, hunting and food-gathering began to give way before the advance of settled agriculture. So today the transformation of society by the application of reason, science, and technology is thrusting the old static subsistence economies to the backwaters of the world. The world is, in fact, involved in a single revolutionary process of which our four dominant themes are all a part. In the wealthier lands, the first stage of this transformation has been completed in the emergence of the modern, wealthy, reasonably stable, technologically adept capitalist state. In the poorer lands, the first stage only has opened. The contrast between world wealth and world poverty largely turns upon this lag in time.

Now we must examine the impact of the four changes upon emergent lands—and we should remember again the distinction between poorer lands such as India which are at the same time rich in culture, history, and tradition, and tribal lands, whether in Africa, Australia, or Latin America, which lack even the rudiments of a developed tradition. The biological revolution brought about by a sudden acceleration of the birth-rate could not take place in these countries until colonial rule abolished local wars and until modern medical science and modern sanitation began to save babies and lengthen life. That these changes were introduced *before* the establishment of a modern economy is one of the most fateful differences between East and West, and one to which we will return. But until the second half of the nineteenth century most of these lands still followed the old millennial pattern of a population rising to the limits of production and then falling back into violence, struggle, and death where the limits were surpassed. In tribal life, for instance, when the tribe had eaten up the resources available in its hunting-grounds, it had no alternative but to reduce its numbers by malnutrition and starvation or break out and conquer the lands of other tribes, thereby diminishing the numbers on both sides. This cycle was one of the perennial causes of tribal war.

Even in a great settled civilization like China, history has given us a kind of physical representation of the 'melancholy wheel' of fate in the pressure of population rising to the limit of resources, and there precipitating violence, despair, banditry, civil war, and invasion. Then, under tribulations of all kinds, the population falls back again to numbers which the food supply can carry, only to rise once more as peace is restored—a kind of self-perpetuating cycle in which the wheel of fate is driven by pressure of population into a constant alternation of peaceful growth and violent diminution. This, until the day before yesterday, seemed to be the fundamental fatality of man's existence.

Now let us turn to the second force: the new revolutionary emphasis on work and effort devoted to the things of *this* world, the drive of interest devoted to changing and bettering man's physical environment. In traditional or tribal societies, this force is, in the main, lacking. Very largely, the material organization of life and, above all, the natural sequence of birth and death, of the seasons, of planetary change, have been taken as given: they were not the subject of speculative activity. In primitive tribal society one can say that nature is very largely accepted as impenetrable by reason. It can be propitiated. It can be worked on by human will through magic. A flood may be diverted by drowning a male child. But no one connects the precipitation of rain at the head of the watershed with the expected annual flow and devises earthworks to avert disaster. Life is lived in the midst of mystery which cannot be manipulated, beyond very narrow limits, in answer to human needs.

In the great archaic societies—of Babylon, of Egypt, of the Indus Valley, or of the Yellow River—both the exploration of reality and the use of technology registered a formidable advance. Irrigation works such as those of ancient Egypt demanded elaborate scientific calculation, accurate observation of nature, and efficient, large-scale administration. And societies which evolved astronomy and the mathematical sciences to the levels

(43)

THE RICH NATIONS AND THE POOR NATIONS

achieved by the Persians or the Greeks achieved a pene-
tration of matter by the human intellect unequalled
until our own day. But the dynamism of our modern
interest in created things was lacking. In some societies,
as we shall see, the lack followed from a certain scientific
indifference; in others, from a dissociation between the
understanding of natural law and any idea of using the
laws as tools for experimental work; and in all societies
from a static concept of life in which the chief means
of subsistence—agriculture—provided daily bread for
the many and magnificence for the few, but was not a
capital resource to be steadily extended by further investment. And, in truth, once the limits of land and
water were reached, lack of scientific experiment in-
hibited further expansion.

In short, the chief aims of these societies were not
this-worldly in our modern sense. Take, for instance,
the significant Victorian phrase 'making good.' We understand it in terms of making money, of achieving material success in the broadest sense. In pre-modern
society no such meaning could possibly have been at-
tached to any activity thought of as being 'good.' In
tribal society, approved behaviour implies strict observ-
ance of tribal laws and customs. In archaic civilization,
the good man, the man of wisdom, is the man who ob-
serves the rules and duties of his way of life: the rich
man, in magnificence, affability, and alms-giving; the
poor man, in work and respect. No group, except the
despised merchant, devotes his life to accumulation.
And even the merchant tends, as he did in China, to

turn his wealth into land and leave the life of capital-formation behind as soon as his fortune permits the change. Such societies incline of their very nature to be backward-looking, to preserve rather than to create, and to see the highest wisdom in the effort to keep things as they are. Under these conditions no under-lying psychological drive impels people to work and accumulate for the future. Wisdom is to wait on Provi-dence and follow in the ways of your forefathers, ways of life compatible with great serenity, great dignity, profound religious experience, and great art, but not with the accumulation of material wealth for society as a whole.

The lack of the third revolution—equality—has worked in the same sense. There was no concept of equality in traditional society. As one knows from still-existing tribal societies, leadership lies with the old men of the tribe. There is no way for the 'young men' to claim equality. They simply have to wait for the years to pass. Seniority (as in the American Senate) also ensures that the leaders are men who respect the backward-looking traditions of the group and have a vested interest in the unequal prestige conferred by advancing years. It is the inescapable recipe for extreme conservatism.

When tribal society is left behind, the values sup-ported by the leaders are still conservative. They are fixed by an inviolate upper order. Save in times of im-mense upheaval, the peasant does not reach the throne. King, warrior, landlord form a closed order to which recruitment is in the main by birth. In India the fixedness of the pattern extended to everyone. A man is born to his caste and to no other. The very idea of equality is almost meaningless since you are what you are and you cannot measure yourself against other men who are entirely different by birth and by caste. Caste thus reinforced the inability of the merchant class to achieve greater influence and status. The merchant remained a Vaishya—the merchant caste—and money-making was not considered a valuable enough occupation to warrant any increase in status or esteem. Thus the Indian merchant did not achieve the political break-through which launched the rising power of the middle classes in Western Europe.

Another facet of equality—a vital facet for economic growth—was lacking: since there was no national community as we understand it, competitive drives based on national equality were also absent. The tribe is a sort of tiny nation, a nation in embryo, but it cannot exercise the same economic influence as the modern nation because it is too small to be a significant market. In any case, tribal agriculture is devoted to subsistence, not to exchange.

The larger post-tribal political units were, in the main, dynastic or imperial units—one thinks of such loose structures as the India of the Guptas or of China's gigantic bureaucracy—in which there was little interconnection between the scattered cities and the great mass of people living their isolated, subsistence village lives. Certainly there was not enough economic and social coherence to define a market in such terms that a merchant would feel himself in competition with other vigorous national markets and could operate with driving energy to defend national interests against the rival national interests of others. The competitive 'equality' of Western Europe's commerce was wholly absent. As one sees again and again in human history—or in daily life—people do not begin to act in new ways until they have formulated the idea of such ways in their minds. The idea of the nation was immensely reinforced—but also in part created—by the rivalry of commercial interests in Western Europe.

Now we turn to the last and most pervasive of the revolutions, the crucial revolution of science and saving. There is virtually no science in tribal society. There is a good deal of practical experience, skilled work, and early technique. It seems possible, for instance, that primitive farming developed as a result of close observation of nature's cycle of seed and harvest and its imitation in fertility rites and religious festivals. But the idea of controlling material things by grasping the inner law of their construction is absent. An underlying sense of the mysteriousness of things explains, as we have noticed, the use of magic. But magic depends on the force of a man's will, not upon the nature of the things upon which he tries to exercise his will. And since the human will is a very potent force, one occasionally encounters some very strange and unaccountable results which seem inexplicable in ordinary terms. Few travellers return from Africa without some sense of having brushed the uncanny fringes of a world where some of the ordinary rules do not apply. Nonetheless, primitive society lacks the sustained and purposive manipulation of matter for human ends which becomes possible once you grasp the laws to which matter responds.

In great traditional civilizations such as India and China, there certainly was enough intellectual ferment for a vast scientific break-through to be theoretically possible. Many of the most acute minds in those societies devoted themselves to systematic thought for generations. In the Eastern Mediterranean, among the Chaldeans and the Egyptians, some of the basic mathematical tools of science had been forged long before the Christian era. Yet the break-through never came. In India, there could be no obsessive research into material things since many of the finest spirits thought of the natural world as in some sense an illusion with no fundamental significance for human beings. In China, for a rather different reason, science failed to achieve the pre-eminence one might have expected in one of the most brilliantly intellectual societies of all time; and one in which printing—and gunpowder—were invented far ahead of the West. The reason is one more illustration of the degree to which revolutions begin—or fail to begin—in the minds of men. The Confucian gentleman who dominated the official thinking of Chinese society thought science an occupation for charlatans and fools and, therefore, not really respectable. One need hardly add that if the best brains do not think a pursuit respectable, the best brains do not devote their time to it.

The Confucians had an excuse for their prejudice. In

Europe, the medieval alchemists spent much of their time and energy trying to discover the 'philosopher's stone'—the catalyst which would turn base metals into gold. In the course of their futile search they made many sound experimental discoveries about the properties of metals and some people regard them as precursors of the inductive and experimental methods upon which modern science is based.

In China the 'philosopher's stone' took another form —the 'elixir of life.' China's emperors did not want gold. They wanted immortality and at their courts the Taoists, followers of a mystical and metaphysical religious 'way,' conducted practical experiments with plants and chemicals to see if the elixir could be produced in a test-tube. To the Confucians, the folly of the aim overshadowed the potential value of the means. They turned their backs on experiment and, in doing so, on science as well. So in China, for all the ancient glory of its culture, for all the force and vitality of its intellectual tradition, the scientific break-through could not occur.

Primitive and archaic societies match their lack of scientific *élan* by an equal lack of sustained saving. Every society saves something. Saving is, after all, not consuming. If everything were consumed, men would be reduced to hunting and fishing—and even these occupations require rods and spears. But in settled agricultural societies, seed-corn is set aside for the next harvest and men do the hedging and ditching and field-levelling needed to carry production forward year by year. Probably such saving for maintenance and repair

—and more occasionally by land-clearing and irrigation, for expansion—does not surpass four or five per cent of national income in any year.

The savings which make possible a general change in the techniques of productivity—more roads, more ports, more power, more education, more output on the farms, new machines in the factories—must rise dramatically above the five-per-cent level. Economists fix a level of about twelve to fifteen per cent of national income as the range needed to cover all possible increases in population, some increase in consumption, and a high, expanding level of investment. And no traditional society ever reached this level.

One reason for this fact takes us back to the revolution of equality. The merchant in the Orient never achieved decisive political influence. There were no city corporations, no charters based on autonomous rights. As a result, the merchant never achieved full security either. The government of kings and emperors was a government above the law, depending upon the monarch's whim. There is a brilliant phrase used by one of the young gentlemen of the East India Company to describe the uncertainties of the commercial calling in India. He describes the monarch and his tax-gatherers as bird's-nesters who leave a merchant to accumulate a nestful of eggs and then come to raid them all. One can well understand that under such conditions the stimulus to sustained capital accumulation is fairly marginal. On the contrary, the tendency is to put money that is earned from trade—and a great deal of money was earned—either into hoards of currency that can be hidden or else into jewels which are easily transportable and easily hid. But neither of these reserves makes for the expansion of productive enterprise.

In short, the chief point that distinguishes tribal and traditional society is that all the internal impulses to modernization have been largely lacking. And yet today these societies are everywhere in a ferment of change. How has this come about? Where did the external stimulus come from? There is only one answer. It came, largely uninvited, from the restless, changing, rampaging West. In the last 300 years, the world's ancient societies, the great traditional civilizations of the East, together with the pre-Iberian civilizations of Latin America and the tribal societies of Africa, have all, in one way or another, been stirred up from outside by the new, bounding, uncontrollable energies of the Western powers which, during those same years, were undergoing concurrently all the revolutions—of equality, of nationalism, of rising population, and of scientific change—which make up the mutation of modernization.

The great world-wide transmitter of the modernizing tendency has been without doubt—for good and evil —Western colonialism. It is typical, I think, of the way in which the changes have come about that, again and again, Western merchants were the forerunners of upheaval. They went out to bring back the spices and silks and sophistications of the Orient to cold and uncomfortable Europe. At first, they had no intentions of conquering anything. They simply tried to establish

(51)

monopoly positions for themselves—hardly surprising when you could earn a 5,000-percent profit on a shipload of nutmeg making landfall in Europe—and to drive the traders of other nations away. They fought each other ferociously at sea but on land controlled only 'factories'—clusters of warehouses, port installations, and dwelling houses held on sufferance from the local ruler. And so the position might have remained. But Dutch pressure was too great for the frail political structure of Java in the seventeenth century and little by little, by backing compliant sultans and deposing sullen ones, the Dutch became political masters of all the rich 'spice islands.'

In the following century, the Mogul superstructure collapsed in India and in their maneuvering to destroy French influence the British found themselves assuming power by a similar route, first backing local contenders, then, saddled with them as puppets or incompetents, gradually assuming the power which slipped from their enfeebled grip. The Europeans had come out to trade. Imperial control was a by-product—and an increasingly ruinous one in commercial terms—yet as late as 1850 the nominal ruler in India was still a merchant corporation—'John Company,' the East India Company.

Colonial control, developing from its origins in trade, began to set the whole revolution of modernization into motion. It launched the radical changes brought about by a rapidly increasing growth in population. Western control introduced the beginnings of medical science.

It ended internal disorder. A crowding into the big cities began. There were some attempts at more modern sanitation.

Towards the close of the nineteenth century a spurt of population began throughout India and the Far East. But this spurt had a different consequence from the comparable increase in the West. Western lands were relatively under-populated—North America absolutely so—when the processes of modernization began. The growth in numbers was a positive spur to economic growth; it brought labourers into the market and widened the market. At the same time the new machines, the new developing economy based on rising productivity, expanded the possibilities of creating wealth in a way that more than outstripped the growth in population. But in the Far East, in India, where population was already dense, the effect of the colonial impact was to increase the rate of the population's growth without launching a total transformation of the economy. More births, longer lives, sent population far beyond the capabilities of a stumbling economy. Today the grim dilemma has appeared that population is so far ahead of the means of satisfying it that each new wave of births threatens in each generation to wipe out the margin of savings necessary to sustain added numbers. The West, where growth in population acted as a spur to further expansion, has not faced this dilemma, and in the East it is not yet clear how so grave a dilemma *can* be faced.

Colonial rule brought in the sense of a this-worldly

concern for the advantages of material advance by the simplest and most direct route—the 'demonstration effect.' The new merchants, the new administrators, lived better, lived longer, had demonstrably more materially satisfying lives. The local people saw that this was so and they began to wonder why and whether others might not live so too. Above all, the local leaders saw vividly that the new scientific, industrial, and technological society enjoyed almost irresistible power. This, too, they naturally coveted.

At the same time, the colonial system did set in motion some definite beginnings in the processes of technical change and economic growth. There was some education of local people in the new techniques of Western life. Some merchants in the old societies, the Compradors in China, for instance, or the Gujaratis in India, began to exercise their talents as entrepreneurs in a new, settled, commercial society. Some of the preliminaries of industrialization—railways, ports, roads, some power —the preliminaries we call 'infrastructure'—were introduced to the benefit of the new colonial economy. Some export industries expanded to provide raw materials for the West. Virtually nothing was done about basic agriculture; but plantation systems did develop agricultural products—tea, pepper, ground-nuts, jute —for the growing markets of Europe.

Above all, the new political ideas streamed in. Western education gave an *élite* a first look at Magna Charta. In their school-books in India the sons of Indians could read Edmund Burke denouncing the depradations of

Englishmen in India. The new sense of equality, inculcated by Western education, was reinforced by the daily contrast between the local inhabitants and the colonial representatives who claimed to rule them. Personal equality fused with the idea of national equality, with the revolt educated men increasingly felt at being run by another nation. The whole national movement of anti-colonialism was stirred up by Western ideas of national rights and national independence, and by the perpetual evidence that the rights were being denied.

Everywhere there was ferment; everywhere there was the beginning of change; everywhere a profound sense that the old ways were becoming inadequate, were in some way no longer valid or viable for modern man. And this feeling stirred up an equally violent reaction. Men rose up to say that the old ways were better and that the new-fangled fashions would destroy all that was valuable and profound in indigenous civilization. Between the modernizers and the traditionalists, between the young men who wanted to accept everything and the old men who wanted to reject everything, the local community threatened to be distracted by contradictory leadership. A crisis of loyalty and comprehension superimposed itself on all the other crises. It was rare for a country to achieve the national coherence that was achieved in India under the leadership of Gandhi in whom ancient vision and the modern idea of equality could coexist, and around whom old and new were thus able to unite.

The important point to remember, however, if one

wishes to grasp the present contrast between the rich nations and the poor, is that all these changes, introduced pell-mell by colonialism, did not really produce a new and coherent form of society, as they had done in the West. There was no 'take-off,' to use Professor Rostow's phrase, into a new kind of society. The colonial impact introduced problems that seemed too large to be solved, or, at least, problems that offered immense difficulty to any solution. Take, for instance, the problem of population. You could not deny medicine; you could not resist sanitation; yet all the time life lengthened, the birth-rate went on going up, and you could almost watch population beginning to outstrip resources that were not growing in proportion because saving and capital formation were still inadequate. Yet the rising population continuously made saving more difficult.

This small level of saving meant that all economic developments under colonialism—or semi-colonialism —were on too small a scale to lead to a general momentum. China is a good example. After the Opium Wars the British compelled the crumbling Manchu Empire to open its ports to Western trade. In the so-called treaty ports, quite a rapid rate of economic and industrial expansion took place. Europeans brought in capital. Some Chinese entrepreneurs joined them. International trade soared. The customs, also under European control, grew to be an important source of revenue. Plans for building railways were prepared. Meanwhile, however, the desperate, over-crowded countryside where the bulk of the people lived slipped steadily down into deeper ruin. Little economic activity could spread beyond the Westernized areas; for there were no markets, no savings, no initiative—only the dead weight of rural bankruptcy.

Similarly, in India the only areas where anything like a sustained 'take-off' began to occur were in the neighbourhood of Bombay with its shrewd merchants and great port, among the Scottish jute-growers round Calcutta, and with the lively, adaptable farmers of the Punjab. Elsewhere, the countryside was largely unaffected by the new economic forces.

The same patchiness affected social life and education. All over Asia the educational system began to produce an *élite* who believed in Western ideas of law, Western ideas of liberty, of constitutional government. But behind them there was little general change among the people at large and, above all, no trace of change in the vast number—eighty or more per cent of the population—who lived on the land where the old, unchanged, subsistence agriculture went on as before. And so there came about what one can only call a kind of dual society, in which the scattered growing-points of a modern way of life were restrained almost to the pitch of immobility by enormous forces of inertia inherent in the old framework of society.

When, for instance, one reads of the attempts made by small groups of Chinese merchants in the late nineteenth century to transform their economy in such a way that they could withstand the commercial and political pressure of the West, one confronts again and again the fact that the real society simply had not changed enough to go along with them. The Court was backward-looking. The Confucian bureaucracy was still utterly unchanged. Worse still, the merchants themselves were still divided in their own minds. They still hankered for the days when a successful merchant naturally put all his capital into land and became a member of the landed gentry. At every point, there were psychological blocks in men's minds when it came to completing the changes they had been ready to start. In a very real sense societies like China or India in the last century were caught between a world that had died and a new world that could not yet be born—and this is, of course, the perfect recipe for maximum psychological and social strain.

Perhaps one can best judge the extent of the inhibitions by examining the opposite example of Japan. There, an extraordinarily efficient and ruthless ruling class determined, after the forced opening of their ports by the Western Powers, to transform their country completely on the modern Western model. They decided that nothing short of almost total technical transformation would give them power to resist the West. So they forced through the reform of agriculture, the imposition of savings on the people, the absolute liquidation of all forms of the feudal economy. They introduced industry, sent many men to train abroad, and set in motion a drive for universal literacy. Although, unhappily, they also borrowed from the contemporary West a spirit of imperialism also present in their own traditions, they were able to transform their society radically in about thirty years and eliminated the social blocks and psychic inhibitions which held the other societies miserably suspended between contradictory worlds.

But elsewhere throughout the uncommitted world, in the traditional societies of China and India, in large parts of Latin America, and in the primitive emergent countries of Africa, old and new remained locked in a kind of battle, stuck fast in an apparently unbreakable deadlock. And how to break out of it; how to get the forces of modernization flowing through all of society; how to change leadership; how to get the new cadres in education; how to stimulate massive saving; how to get agriculture transformed: all these urgent and irresistible problems of the new society still wait to be answered.

This is a fact which the West cannot ignore. Most of the dilemmas of the under-developed areas have been stirred up by Western impact. Yet I think it is not entirely untrue to say that the Western powers are not looking very hard to find answers to these dilemmas. And this, I think, is for a very good reason. They have largely forgotten about their own transition. They are not conscious of the fact that a hundred years ago, even fifty years ago, many of them were struggling with just these problems of changing leadership, of developing new social groups, giving rights to new classes, finding methods of achieving greater saving, and securing a technological break-through on a massive scale. We take our development so much for granted that we hardly understand the dilemmas of those who have not yet travelled so far.

Another reason for our relative indifference is that owing to the relative under-population of our part of the world and owing to the scale of latent resources waiting to be developed in the Atlantic world, we in the West had not too difficult a passage to modernity; certainly nothing compared with the really appalling dilemmas that are faced by the under-developed world today. So, although we are perhaps beginning to see that they face almost insurmountable problems, I do not think that we have worked out our response or even perhaps fully measured our responsibility. Yet there is no human failure greater than to launch a profoundly important endeavour and then leave it half done. This is what the West has done with its colonial system. It shook all the societies in the world loose from their old moorings. But it seems indifferent whether or not they reach safe harbour in the end.

This is one difficulty; but there is another, a greater one. While we face these dilemmas, another set of answers to them has been formulated—also in the West. It claims to go to the heart of all these revolutions and offer a surer route to equality, to material well-being, to the achievement of technology, science, and capital. Communism claims to be the pattern of the future and to hold the secret of the next phase of history for mankind. In one sense, the claim is serious. Communism *is* a sort of résumé of the revolutions that make up modernization and it offers a method of applying them speedily to societies caught fast in the dilemmas of transition. We must, therefore, admit that, at the present moment, the poor nations, the uncommitted nations, face a double challenge. They face an enormous challenge of change. But, in addition, they face an equally vast challenge of choice.

Chapter Three

Communism's Blue Print

TODAY about one-third of mankind lives under the political control of Communism, and already I think we can ask the question whether a variety of different kinds of Communism may not be beginning to appear in the world and whether a picture of one vast monolithic Communist bloc may not be disintegrating a little. There is not only the deviant strain of Titoism in Yugoslavia. Even among 'orthodox' Communists the emphasis put on different problems varies. Different methods of dealing with the basic problems of agriculture, for instance, have appeared, varying from the private farms of Poland through the collectivization of Russia to the more extreme communal system of

Titoism

farming in China.

There is, again, a different approach to the problems of war, and of the Cold War. It seems possible that China, at an earlier stage of its revolution, is more anxious to stir up trouble abroad than is Russia where forty years' painful construction is at stake. And there may be an even more fundamental divergence. Although we do not yet know what its consequences will be, there is surely a clear distinction between the Communism of the relatively rich in such countries as Russia or Czechoslovakia, and the Communism of the desperately poor that we find in China. When the Chinese Communist revolution exploded, it was against a background of gross over-population in a land where the per-capita income was probably below $60 a year. It seems quite clear to me that the kind of society that can develop in Russia on the basis of relatively low population and extraordinarily rich resources may well move steadily away from the forms of a society struggling, as in China, with gross poverty and an extreme pressure of population.

Bearing these differences in mind, we must nevertheless try to define Communism and one way would be to say that it is an attempt to put all the revolutions of our day into one coherent system. But before following up this approach we have to see that one of our revolutions is missing—the biological revolution of explosively rising population. So far as this crisis is concerned, official Communism neglects it, disregards it, and in fact claims that it is no problem.

For the Russians, Malthus might never have written. His basic thesis—that the growth of population would tend at some point to outstrip resources—is simply dismissed as a reflection of a basic inability to understand the inadequacies of capitalism and as a fundamental defeatism before the bright prospects of the future.

Nor is this simply a theoretical attitude. In China, for a time in 1957, some effort was made to persuade people to limit the size of their families. But the campaign came to an abrupt end, in spite of an annual growth in population of some twelve million souls. Thereafter the general line seems to have been that the problem of over-population or of potential over-population is bound up, not with basic biological facts, but simply with the inadequacy of capitalism to cope with it.

But all the other revolutions of our times are absorbed into Marxism, probably reaching there a pitch of coherence, of drive, and of unity unique in human history. Take, first of all, our revolution of materialism. In the West, materialism has taken the form certainly of an enormous interest in the natural order and of a determined attempt to penetrate its secrets by means of science. It has taken, too, the form of a strong commitment to the possibility of better conditions on earth and a belief that man has the right, the privilege, even the duty, to better material conditions, both for himself and for his fellow men. But it has certainly not led to a total disbelief in, and rejection of, any other order of reality. Our societies are plural in thought, plural in their ideals, plural in their ways of approaching reality.

Communism attempts, on the contrary, to make materialism the measure of all things. The basic physical techniques, economic forms, and property relations of society are held to be the determinant factors in fixing all other aspects of human reality—art, philosophy, religion. This anchoring of all phenomena in a supposedly definable and explorable material base is what, in Marxist claims, gives the system alone the right to be called scientific; and it enables Marxism to predict 'objectively' the course of history by examining the material forces which will compel it to behave as it does. This, incidentally, is why to this day all anti-social behaviour in Russia tends to be attributed to the remaining traces of capitalism. The blame could not lie with Socialist institutions which are, by definition, incapable of projecting evil results.

Nonetheless, the materialist base supports a Messianic hope. This Marx achieves by attributing all the faults and errors of society to the institution of private property. The jealousies, the envies, the obstructions to which it gives rise drive society forward on an ever-renewed cycle of discontent, in which once-dominant classes are succeeded by new groups thrusting upwards until at last the workers, rejecting private property, take over and set up a classless society where the lion will lie down with the lamb and all the evils of the world will pass away.

This is, I think, all highly theoretical and it is my impression that in Communist education these days much of the dogma is accepted unthinkingly and slips very much to the back of people's minds. What is left is perhaps not so much an elaborate ideology as a general attitude of mind which regards the achievements of the kingdoms of this world as the most important issue for man and which looks on Communism as the key to the future. It includes considerable distrust of other forms of society since, by definition, capitalism is wicked and obsolete. Perhaps above all, it conveys the feeling of moving forward to a vision of world-order, to a final consummation of history which gives a Messianic turn to life and a sense of excitement to the road ahead. I do not suggest all Communists share the hope. Indeed, there is evidence that a certain boredom with the high imperatives seems to be fairly widespread among young people. As with religion in the West, the appeal may be intense only to an *élite*. One can also doubt whether this strange transformation of materialism into a kind of religion is as crucial as other aspects of Communism. Yet dreams are dreams and men cannot live without them. We would be unwise to underestimate the potency of Communism's dream of a world made one and equal and rich.

When we turn to the revolution of equality we see that it is, of course, central to Communism. It claims to provide the consummation of all equality. Men and nations alike will be organized on the principle: 'from each according to his capacities, to each according to his needs.' This principle, it will be noticed, not only eliminates all class differences; it tries to establish a fundamental norm of 'need' which applies to every

Strange transformation of materialism

human being and should, in theory, do away with all differences in reward and status based on performance or special talent. Such a 'norm' has been tried successfully in human history. It is the basis of monasticism, Christian or Eastern, and is rooted in the rejection of personal possessions of any kind. But Communism assumes that the intense religious dedication which makes monastic communalism possible can be spread to the whole civil community.

At first, a violent cataclysm will bring down the mighty from their seat and exalt them of low degree— the old Biblical phrase is strictly relevant. Thereafter, however, the course is less clear. What we have seen of Communist society so far suggests the force of George Orwell's warning that whereas 'all animals are equal, some animals are more equal than others.' Certainly, we have seen in actual Communist societies that those who control power—the bureaucrats, the organization men—secure for themselves social differences, both in wealth and in opportunity, which are at least equivalent to the kind of class distinctions we have in the West. Indeed, they may in some areas be wider since the base of society is still so desperately low. To have command of a car in a society where there are virtually no cars confers greater privilege than does the manager's Cadillac in the West. The gap between top executive and floor-cleaner is almost certainly larger in Soviet society because the whole community has not yet reached the affluence of mass consumption. Milan Djilas, the dissident Yugoslav leader and writer, goes farther and suggests that 'the new class' of bureaucrats will be self-perpetuating since its children will be born to privileges denied to others and start as an *élite* enjoying all the unequal advantages wealthy children enjoy in the West.

However, Communism as an order of society is not yet fifty years old. Its future rigidities and encrustations can be guessed at but not confirmed. What is certain is that its primary appeal *before* it takes power is to those whom the existing social order disappoints or oppresses. Rising young sons of the middle class who see power remain with traditional feudal leaders; workers herding miserably into cities in the first 'push' of primary capital accumulation; above all, the dispossessed on the land: these make up the cadres and the mass following of the Communist upsurge.

When, however, we come to the question of *national* equality under Communism, the situation is not so clear. In theory, certainly all nations are equal and none may oppress or control another. One of the most striking first gestures of the Bolshevik revolution in Russia was to announce the liberation of all central-Asian subject peoples brought into the Russian empire by the Tsarist régime: Kazakhs, Uzbeks, Armenians, Kirghiz. But then the ambivalence begins. Communism also teaches that nationalism is simply a projection of the capitalist *bourgeois* phase of human development; and, as we have seen, there *is* some link between the definition of market and the definition of the nation. When, therefore, Communists argue, mankind passes beyond capitalist economics, it will leave nationalism behind as well. Nationalism, as a restrictive and dividing device, will come to an end in the classless, nationless world order which Communism will bring about. This change need not suppress national culture; and indeed, national differences of culture and language must be respected. Yet nationalism should be understood as a passing phase.

This, in shorthand, is the theory. When it comes to practice, the outlook is much more complex. Even if in strict theory nationalism is primarily a projection of the *bourgeois* phase of development, the Communists have been quick to see how intense nationalism can become in under-developed and pre-*bourgeois* communities, provided they have come under colonial control. Societies at very varied stages of growth can catch the nationalistic epidemic, since nationalism is the driving force behind the movement to end Western colonial control—what the Communists call 'the old imperialist order.' They are ready to support local nationalists in Africa or Latin America—men such as Castro or Sekou Touré—if by that means they can hasten the end of Western influence. Such local leaders do not have to be Communist. They may, like Nasser, keep their own Communists under lock and key. The Communists are not perturbed. End Western influence first, they argue, and then we can adopt new tactics. Meanwhile, we say 'Yes' to local nationalism as a means of ending the old Western forms of rule and influence.

Communists would also, whatever the theory, admit

the usefulness of nationalism as a means of rallying the people to support an accomplished Communist revolution. In Russia, devotion to the Russian image, in China dedication to Chinese strength, is obviously used in the effort to win people to the revolutionary régime. Particularly during the devastating impact of Hitler's attack upon Russia, the sense of Holy Russia, of Great Russia, of all its history, all its glory, all its resistances and victories was drawn on fully to rally its citizens to the defence of the Soviet Union.

So far, then, nationalism, whatever the underlying stages of economic development, can be legitimate in Communist eyes. But now comes the paradox. One of the basic facts in world Communism today is that the doctrine has taken root in two immensely powerful and imperialist states—states which have, over the centuries, absorbed millions of citizens of other tribes and races. What of the nationalism of these groups? Suppose it does not wither away as a result of economic development under Communist discipline? Can it be fostered and supported? Clearly not; for, on the analogy of self-determination elsewhere, it might weaken Soviet or Chinese control. So we reach the ambivalence that nationalism is good in Ghana or Cuba or Iraq, but bad in Hungary or Kirghizia or Tibet. Nationalisms may, like men, all be equal; but some, clearly, are 'more equal' than others; none more so than in Russia or China. The Russians dismiss the stirrings inside their own frontiers as 'bourgeois vestiges.' Yet in 1932, as the horrors of collectivization grew, it proved necessary to shoot most of the cabinet of the Ukraine for these same 'vestiges.' And in all our memories the tragedy of Hungary is still vivid: the desire of a perfectly coherent self-conscious European nation to throw off Russian control led first to an uprising of the whole people and then to its brutal suppression by the Russians. There could be no more striking illustration of the fundamental inequality between national groups within the Soviet sphere. Nor do I think that we have yet seen the end of the possible permutations and combinations of this ambivalence.

Where the Communists incorporate the revolutions of our day into their system with least equivocation is in the sphere of science, savings, and technology. Science is welcomed as the basic secret of successful existence. Marx, as we have remarked, always claimed that his Communism, unlike the visionary Socialism of his contemporaries, was the truly scientific Communism. Only Communism uncovered the inner laws that explain the workings of human society and human classes, just as such laws as those of thermodynamics explain the workings of solids and masses. In a sense, this is simply a variant of nineteenth-century rationalism— indeed of some types of philosophy today—which accepts only one form of meaning and validity: the form which can be checked by the measuring and calculating techniques of science. Western thought today is perhaps more inclined to accept the limits of this approach, while giving full value to the astonishing results it can give in its appropriate field. In the Soviet Union, one can imagine that the uninhibited acceptance of science as the key to everything gives an extra edge of energy to its pursuit of scientific objectives. Certainly, a nation that has produced the Sputnik and photographed the dark side of the moon possesses an incomparable thrust of scientific energy; and in Soviet education, emphasis on science has already produced a society capable of mobilizing more scientific and technical skills than perhaps any other—certainly at a comparable stage of development.

But this scientific break-through in Russia would have been impossible if the Soviet Union had not also directly developed into a highly capitalist state—state-capitalism, but capitalism nonetheless. The vast accumulation of savings in the decades of the Plans permitted the equally vast expansion of education. Without capital, schools and universities could not have multiplied; without the trained minds the economic system could not have expanded. In fact, as we see now, Communism's present strength depends more on its educational thrust than on any other single early development.

Nevertheless it is worth looking for a moment to the pendant development, the forceful accumulation of capital, for it goes to the roots of Marxism. Marx believed fundamentally that the capitalists would first create an industrial society and that the Communists would then take it over as a going concern. And he had a reason for seeing this as an historically inevitable process. He derived it quite simply from his direct ob-

MARX: CAPITALISTS TO CREATE AN INDST SOCTY
COMUNISTS TO TAKE OVER

servation of the first stages of the first industrial break-through in Britain. Private capitalists, private merchants, private entrepreneurs invented the capitalist system; they did not know they were doing so; they thought they were making profits. But it was their desire for profits that drove the whole system forward and was, in the context of Britain's new unified national market, a most effective method of promoting economic expansion. The man who makes profits is the man who organizes the production of some goods or service in such a way that people are prepared to give up more resources to procure it than he put into it in the first place. And the better he organizes his resources, the larger the margin between costs and the price people are ready to pay for the goods. This margin is his profit-margin and it is then available for further investment, for creating new tools in the economy, for making experiments in new goods and in new types of technology. Moreover, at a time when labour is plentiful, unorganized, and weak, the cost element of wages can be held down and profits will be proportionately greater. As we have already noticed, in the early nineteenth century British workers were in this condition. Their wages were subsistence wages. The extra surplus was available for even more capital investment. The 'big push' in investment was helped by the failure of the workers' consumption to rise in the first decades of industrialization.

This was the condition that chiefly impressed Marx. He regarded all profits as exploitation; he did not deny their role in releasing further resources for further investment; such was the historic task of the *bourgeoisie*. But he believed the process could not last because of an essential contradiction. Although the new machines were able to pour out more and more goods, wages would remain low and people's purchasing power would not grow to meet the output of the machines. There would be crises of over-production—which were really crises of under-consumption—and this would involve the system in ever deepening instability and contradiction. Further, Marx believed—for reasons sufficiently fantastic for us not to go into them here—that wages would actually fall and that people would get poorer. And as the mass of the people grew poorer, a shrinking number of 'monopolists'—the organizers, the profit-makers—would grow richer, and in the end the whole society would relapse into a revolutionary conflict in which the vast mass of the poor would cast out the small body of the rich, take over the industrial machine which the monopolists had built, and establish a classless, profitless society—which would be Communism.

As we know, the snag to Marx's theory lay in the fact that as the nineteenth century advanced, the workers began to share more adequately in the new society's wealth. Far from going down, their real wages went up. They began to organize, to exploit their position as voters, and to agitate for what we now call the welfare state. They began to have a stake in the new kind of society which Marx had not foreseen and which contradicted his basic assumptions. He died with the

contradiction unresolved. Lenin took it up and dis-
covered—at least to his own satisfaction—that the reason why there had been a greater sharing of wealth in
the West, even with the workers, was that the wealth
had been filched from the Western colonies. The colonial workers were now bearing the full brunt of the
industrial revolution and carrying on their sweated
backs not only Western 'monopolists' but Western trade
unionists. One consequence of this discovery was that
Lenin put very much greater emphasis on the revolt
of the colonies against Western imperial supremacy
and came to believe that the way to the West would
lie through Peking and Delhi.

Another aspect of his theory also deserves notice. He
believed that Western capitalists had to invest abroad
since the failure of internal consumption to increase
limited the scope for further profitable investment at
home. Seeking hungrily for profits, they would entrench
themselves in foreign lands, either directly or through
local puppets, then fight to keep everybody else out of
their preserves. This was the essential link between
capitalism, colonialism, and war; and the twist Lenin's
interpretation gave to men's thinking about colonies
survives to this day. In ex-colonial lands it is not un-
usual to find leaders who are highly suspicious of all
forms of private foreign investment on the grounds that
it must entail foreign control and could even involve the
territory in war. This old preconceived idea is stronger
than the new fact that the Western economy, having
translated itself to a new base of high consumption, no

longer has capital to spare and the danger is not 'exploitation' but that capital will simply not be forthcoming for overseas development.

Establishing why Western workers were no longer revolutionary still left Lenin with the problem of what to do about a proletariat no longer ready to act as the vanguard of revolt. He met the problem by evolving the idea of the party as a small secret core with total discipline dedicated to cajoling or compelling the majority to accept its revolutionary leadership. In the conditions of the early twentieth century, Lenin's instrument proved more potent than any mass movement. Even after the agonies of war, Western workers remained fundamentally unrevolutionary. But in Russia the war went like a steam-roller over the beginnings of modernization. And it was in this disintegrating society that the small, highly restricted conspiratorial group of Bolsheviks took over power and set up the first government in history to be based upon Communism.

At this point the inadequacies of the Marxist analysis became apparent. The Communists were in control. But what they controlled was not a highly evolved industrial society; it was a nation flattened by war and barely emerged from the Middle Ages. In 1917, in 1921, and for years after, the great problem in Russia was how to build Communism in a society for which capitalists had not obligingly built the industrial structure in advance. Lenin died with the dilemma unresolved and it was the lot of Stalin to take the formidable and unprecedented decision to achieve a fully developed Western type of industrial community; not by taking it over from the capitalists, but by building it himself—in short, to use the state to do the job which the capitalists had done in the West.

Fortunately for Stalin it was by this time fairly clear how the government could undertake such a task. During the First World War, the massive mobilization of men and material by central government for specific tasks had occurred in Britain, Germany, and France; and the West's war economy was in all probability the great model for the first Five Year Plan. As in war, the planners expand the great metal-using industries, which pour out further machines—as the war economy pours out munitions. Total mobilization is achieved by compelling men and materials to fit into the over-all plan of industrial expansion. And savings are produced by seeing to it that only a very small part of what the workers produce ever goes back to them in terms of consumption. Wartime rationing and wartime inflation provided this discipline between 1914 and 1918. Resources were released massively for war. The 'saving' was probably greater than even in the heroic days of primitive accumulation in Britain.

But whereas the early capitalist system in Britain may have saved the classical twelve to fifteen per cent of national income, the harsh disciplines of the Russian Plans drove the figure up to twenty-five and thirty per cent of the national income. Massive savings derived from the work of the people poured into the new industries, into the new developments beyond the Urals, into the vast

expansion of mines, of transport, of education and research. The saving had to come from the people since it
could come from no other source. It came, above all—
as it does in all stages of primitive accumulation—from
the vast mass of the people living on the land. And here
the sufferings which were imposed upon the peasants,
by the effort to draw out of the farms every last margin
of resources that could be transferred to the cities,
culminated in the agonies of collectivization. And to
this day Soviet agriculture has not fully recovered from
the enormous impact of forced saving imposed on it
in the early days.

Let us now examine the full paradox of the first Communist revolution. Communism which should have
come into being by the ineluctable forces of history, by
the revolt of the large working class in a fully developed
industrial economy, was in fact forced through by a
small conspiratorial group in a vast country in which
nearly eighty per cent of the people still lived in a pre-
industrial society. Moreover, the revolution, which was
to have liberated the workers and peasants, submitted
them to a discipline of forced saving more rugged than
anything imposed in the unplanned West. And the system which was to be most truly the people's government
took for its first model not so much the developed economy of the West in its peacetime semblance, but the
rigidly organized, centrally controlled economy developed in total war.

Thus, in its first incarnation, the revolution had little

resemblance to Communism as Marx had foreseen it. What it did was to create one of the most formidable concentrations of power, both economic and political, that human history has ever seen. And to this extent it accorded well with the traditions of Russian society; a society in which there had been virtually no older forms of constitutional government, no older forms of plural power, and in which autocracy had always centred in a single man—the Tsar.

As if to reinforce the authoritarian stamp imposed on Communism by the nature of Russian society and the scale of the collapse in 1917, the next great breakthrough of Communism—in China—repeated something of the same pattern. China, too, had received only very partial modernization; and what it had of a modern structure—in industry, in communications—had been ravaged by almost continuous war for fifty years. It was in this broken-down, despairing country on the margins of chaos that the Communists, as a small disciplined group, took over power and then imposed upon it the disciplines of total mobilization. And once again, the pattern fitted the traditions and the history of the country. All through China's millennial record—and no country in the world has so long, so continuous, and so sustained an historical tradition as China—two master institutions preserved the unity of the vast empire: the autocratic emperor and the tough, powerful, efficient, imperial bureaucracy of the Mandarins—the first civil service in the world to be recruited by competitive examination. There are other resemblances. In previous dynasties, the incoming rulers frequently experimented with massive policies of social change such as reorganizing the basis of landholding and nationalizing industry. It can even be argued that Confucianism was to a very real degree a state ideology. However, the chief point of resemblance lies in the degree to which the levers of effective power in China have always remained in the hands of the bureaucrats.

This, then, is the basic paradox of Communism. It does not achieve power by the route foreseen by Marx; nor does it establish a society much resembling his blue print—in so far as he had one. Marx was in fact extremely vague about the shape of his classless utopia. Communism has succeeded in taking over power by the forceful action of a dedicated minority in two great societies of traditionally autocratic stamp which were undergoing the collapse and chaos of disastrous war. After the takeover, the Communists' first task has been not—as Marx expected—to run a working system, but on the contrary, to create it, bringing the nation back from the very verge of chaos and mobilizing it into an effective system of modern power.

How is this actual, practical form of Marxism likely to appeal to the emergent, uncommitted nations? How does this pattern of forced growth, achieved through the central planning power of an autocratic state, appeal to countries caught in the twilight zone between the need for change and the capacity to change in fact? We have to realize that its possibilities of attraction are considerable. We have to remember first that in all the uncommitted lands—in Asia, in Latin America, in large parts of Africa—the processes of change have begun. This is the legacy of colonialism and of the impact of Western trade and expansion. A few local leaders are educated in the new ways. Some industries—usually for export and under foreign ownership—have been established. There are new means of transport and communication. Above all, there is a change in the air. The winds blow in from the world bringing the hint of larger opportunities and better things. As a first step, colonial rule must be ended or has been ended. So much is clear. But what then? How can the bright promises of independence be achieved when, all around, the institutions and inhibitions of the old static society seem to remain more or less intact?

It is to the mood of psychological frustration that Communism can speak. It attacks the traditional leaders of the old society—the old rulers and princes, the old landlords, the entrenched groups in commerce and industry, the men who seem to stand in the way of the emergence of the new forces of modernism. And uncommitted peoples need to be fairly sophisticated to wonder whether the old landlord and the new bureaucrat may not share some of the same vices of absolute power. Communism attacks foreign control; it denounces imperialism. And once again you need a certain sophistication to wonder whether Soviet control over its satellites in Eastern Europe may not itself be a new form of imperialism.

In the economic field, Communism offers an intense

discipline of saving. By compelling people to postpone consumption, it attacks head-on the most difficult task in any society where people live so near the margin of absolute poverty that saving must be an agonizing choice. By removing choice and compelling accumulation, Communism offers a pattern of quick growth. When growth-rates are compared between the United States and the Soviet Union—to the advantage of the Soviets—the Communists can claim that they alone know how to give poor societies that kind of boost to saving without which no economy has any hope of moving forward into the 'take-off' into sustained momentum.

This fundamental strategic claim is enhanced by other advantages. Communism has been shown to be a method of seizing power and of developing a society through the work of a small *élite*, a small group of people. In most of the really under-developed areas, the number of men and women who feel themselves able, educated, and dedicated enough to undertake the making of the new society is necessarily small. There is, therefore, an innate appeal in the idea that a small group acting cohesively can accomplish so much. This attraction is reinforced by a certain bold simplicity in the Marxist determination to explain everything in terms of its revolution. When you struggle between a dying world and a world that will not be born; when everything comes to you bearing the face of confusion; when your old ideals and your new ambitions cannot be made to coincide; when the old is fading and you are not sure that you want it to go; and the new must come but is a long time acoming; when you wander in a twilight zone between ideas and ways of life which seem inherently contradictory—then the appeal of the firm simple explanation is intense and you listen with fascination when men come to you and say: 'We have the prescription for the future; we have the total answer; we can tell you what to do; because, look, we have already done it.' It may be that this simplicity, this bold claim to solve everything, is Communism's greatest attraction; and it is one which we in the West would be very unwise to underestimate.

This, of course, is not the whole story. If we are to measure the appeal of Communism soberly and judge where it is most likely to influence policy-makers in emergent territories, we shall have to look much more closely at the dilemmas and possibilities of development itself, at the actual process of growth through which the developing countries have to pass. The dilemmas are becoming clearer, the questions are now more specifically formulated than they were a decade ago. For instance, how can under-developed countries save upwards of fifteen per cent of their national income when per-capita income is as low as $60 a year? How can the whole field of agriculture, where entrenched ways and ancient methods are most firmly set in popular imagination, be set on a new way of growth? How can farmers be brought to produce more, not only for themselves but for the market as well? Where can capital be found for all the 'infra-structure' of industry, for the pre-conditions of growth itself in the shape of roads and power, transportation and harbours? How can manpower and saving be found for the most decisive element of all in infra-structure: the building up of educated manpower? In the field of industrial expansion, given the fact that resources are always limited, which industries should be developed and which should be neglected? Where is it folly to invest? Where is it wisdom to go forward? Should the aim be a high return on capital immediately? Or is there a case for slower returns aiming ultimately at more balanced growth? All these are perfectly concrete questions which are forced upon the leaders of the under-developed areas the moment independence has been achieved and the unity and enthusiasm of the nationalist struggle begins to fade.

At this point we encounter one more advantage enjoyed by the Communists. They say they have the answers. We in the West may very rightly be dubious about a number of the answers. We do not care to be dogmatic—least of all in the daunting but essential field of agriculture. We cannot, therefore, emulate the confidence of the Communist who comes and says, 'Listen to me and I can tell you what to do.' Now, in so far as this hesitation springs from genuine uncertainty about methods, it is honest and can be met by greater efforts to discover what the answers are. But if it simply reflects the fact that we have little sense of urgency about the developing areas and have not given them the hard thought they deserve, then we can take no credit for our 'pragmatism.' It is simply another name for indifference.

ANOTHER NAME FOR INDIFFERENCE.

(84)

Today, for whatever reason, I think we must admit that many of our answers are not formulated, our general policies are not worked out. And sometimes when I look at this whole emerging group of countries coming out of their struggle for independence and facing realities of economic choice and political decision, I wonder if we realize how fast time is running out, how quickly some of these decisions have to be taken, and how urgent it is for us, in our turn, to formulate our own policies for the poor nations of the world. If we do not have the sense of urgency now, can we be certain it may not be too late?

Chapter Four

The Economics of Development

WE HAVE seen how the great revolutions of our time have worked to create a group of wealthy nations in the North Atlantic arena. Now we must look at their impact upon the economies of the developing nations. In this context, only three of the revolutions come into question: the materialist revolution by which people become concerned with this-worldly affairs; the biological revolution by which population has begun to grow in an unprecedented way; and, last but most important of the great changes, the appli-

cation of capital and science to all the processes of earn-
ing man's daily bread. The fourth of our revolutions—
the revolution of equality—is more concerned with the
problems of statecraft and of political development.
This we will discuss later.

I do not think there is much need to stress the impact
of the revolution of materialism and this-worldliness on
the prospects of development. It is simply a fact of human nature that you do not get what you do not want,
and you do not work for what you cannot imagine.
Whether this drive for material betterment takes the
form of the profit motive in the minds of business men
or a politician's determination to see his country strong
and economically developed, it is an essential spur to
the modernization of the economy. The point is obvious
enough not to need much underlining. Yet it is a useful
reminder that some societies still lack this drive towards
material advance and change. Wherever men and
women still prefer status to economic development and
set more store by traditional privilege and custom than
by the risks and rigours of economic change, capital
and science cannot act as full instruments of development since the leaders will not only be ignorant of how
to apply them. They will also have no wish to do so. The
example of Chinese business men towards the end of
the nineteenth century has already been cited. In the
first stages of a developing business system, one finds
again and again a pull between the desire to use the new
wealth for old forms of privilege—investing in land,
adopting feudal habits—and the opposite desire for

more adventurous ways of further investment to widen the economic base of the whole society. Where the identification of new business with old privilege occurs, it creates a formidable block to further change and creates social frictions which easily lead to widespread popular discontent. Communist propaganda in France between the wars was constantly directed against *les deux cent familles:* the two hundred families who owned the bulk of French industry in interlocking alliance with a small section of the earlier aristocracy. In Latin America, today, the business-feudal pattern is a potent cause of unrest and it seems clear that unless the next corner of development can be turned—to the wider spread of consuming power, the growth of a strong, independent middle class and the systematic construction of a market based on mass demand—such a society is likely to be swept away in a tide of radical left-wing or right-wing revolt.

These blocks occur even though a society has already set in motion the processes of modern development. It can be argued that the chief obstacles lie in a much earlier phase: in primitive tribal societies where development has yet to begin. In Africa, for instance, most of the peoples are still organized on tribal lines. In such communal societies, rights to the fruits of the land can be shared by a very large number of strictly non-working members of the kinship group. Why then should an individual farmer work harder if a flock of his 'sisters and his cousins and his aunts'—and they can really be numbered in dozens in polygamous Africa—may come in and eat up his supplies? The 'extended family' acts as a sort of private welfare state. No man need starve if his kin can maintain him. But equally, if there are more to maintain every time a man's income goes up, his incentives to greater effort finally reach zero.

For these reasons, some observers doubt whether modernization can come quickly in Africa. The leaders want it. This first step towards change has been taken. But the pre-conditions of actively seeking change do not exist among the people at large. This view is almost certainly exaggerated. The peasant farmers of Ghana became the largest cocoa-producers in the world on the simple incentive of cash. The Chagga tribe in Tanganyika have used their communal system to build up a highly effective coffee-producing co-operative. In Kenya, Kikuyu farmers, re-settled on viable farms, are producing crops equal to those on white farms. Change is possible. Material incentives do work. But clearly the task is a much longer and more expensive one than in countries of good soil and a progressive farming tradition.

Now we come to what I have called the biological revolution: the enormous acceleration in the rate of growth of the world's population and its possible disproportion to the world's available resources. Many people regard this as the gravest of all mankind's problems and look forward with apprehension to the day, still some centuries ahead, when 'standing-room only' may be the terrestrial rule. I confess that this more distant prospect seems to me somewhat too uncertain for immediate concern. Who knows what changes, maladies, cataclysms, or openings into outer space may not come to modify the strict geometrical progression of population growth? What I want to discuss here is the immediate problem. The increase in population in such areas as Latin America or the Indian subcontinent is such that new mouths threaten to gobble up the margin of fresh savings which alone permits enough capital accumulation for sustained development to become possible. The dilemma is very real. The whole of our modern economy depends upon saving, upon not consuming. But if year after year the population goes on increasing, the number of new mouths coming in to consume can quickly eat up the fresh savings which should have been available for the transformation of the economy. So the question can be restated: Is the rate of population-growth so great that in fact economic development cannot take place?

So far, the answers of history are ambiguous. In Western countries where modernization and rising population went hand in hand, the enormous spurt in population in fact spurred expansion by producing sufficient workers for the new industries and a mass market without which the output of the economy would certainly have been checked.

On the other hand, in tribal or traditional society—for instance, in the great traditional civilization of China—the opposite tendency has been at work. As we have seen, in times of peace the trend is that population climbs to the limits of production. These cannot be further expanded, for science and technology have not yet brought about such astonishing phenomena as the American farmer constantly producing more food from a smaller acreage. At this point, therefore, a melancholy cycle sets in: rising births first eat up the means of living; then starvation and its accompanying disorders set in motion a downward trend. Once population is again below the possible levels of production, there is a restoration of peace and stability which, unhappily for humanity, also brings the return of rising population. This vast, hopeless alternation between the fat years and the lean years can be all too fully documented from the records of Chinese history.

In our own day, which of these two patterns is likely to prevail? One has to remember that the new technology is based on saving. The means of ending the disproportion between people and resources is to apply capital massively to the resources. The difficulty is to secure this massive saving when rising population forces up the levels of consumption. If the rate of increase is two per cent a year—as it is in India, or even three per cent as in parts of Latin America—can people really save on anything like an adequate scale?

By a rough rule of thumb, economists reckon that to secure one unit of income you have to invest three times as much capital. So, even to keep pace with a three-per-cent increase in population, a nation has, roughly speaking, to invest nine per cent of its national income each year. This is well beyond the four to five per cent of traditional society. To get *ahead* of such a birth-rate,

(91)

the rate ought to go up to between twelve and fifteen per cent of national income devoted to productive capital. This is thought to be the central point in achieving a break-through to sustained growth. But can you push savings up to that level, given the original poverty of society? And can you have any hope of doing so if the tide of babies rises faster still?

Communist societies hope to do so by the iron discipline of forced saving. Russia undoubtedly achieved its break-through by this rule; but Russia had no excess population in relation to resources. Scarcity of manpower was the trouble in the early days. China claims to have reached a level of saving in excess of twenty per cent of national income. But we do not yet know whether it has moved decisively ahead. In democratic India, where people are being asked for the first time in history to vote themselves through the tough period of primitive accumulation, savings are lower. Domestic saving is probably not yet ten per cent of national income, although it is rising. But outside capital assistance has raised the proportion to over thirteen per cent. As a result, in spite of a two-per-cent increase in population, India is just keeping ahead. Savings are growing, consumption is a little higher, the vast majority of the people can work and eat. Clearly, however, material progress might have been more rapid if some eighty million more people had not been added to India in the last decade. It is for this reason that Asian governments tend to put increasing emphasis on birth-control as one of the pre-conditions of development.

However, here we have something of a 'hen-and-egg' puzzle. It seems to be an historical fact that nations tend to have the birth-rates they want. For example, in the nineteenth century the French, confronted by new laws on the inheritance of property, opted for smaller families. The Japanese first went through a cycle of very rapid expansion of their population. Now, however, as a result of both personal choice and government legislation, the expansion has ceased and the population seems to be stabilizing. We have to stress the point of choice because we are certainly not suggesting, I take it, that governments should decree what size of families people should have. Their choice will be decisive. And in this context of choice one thing seems clear: that it is when people see more opportunities for better education that they begin to consider whether a smaller family might not be better for themselves and for their children. In other words, I doubt whether one can disentangle the issues of economic development and rising population by any flat argument that stabilization of the population must come first. Lower birth-rates are more likely to be a consequence than a cause of economic expansion. It is above all by the thrust of development and literacy in the modernizing economy that conditions can be achieved in which parents begin to choose smaller families. Governments may assist the choice by encouraging family planning. There will doubtless continue to be considerable moral debate upon the means of limitation. But the decisive point is what millions of parents choose to do; and here, I think, history suggests strongly that a certain amount of modernization must occur before smaller families seem desirable.

This leaves unsolved the problem of securing the original thrust of investment. The Communist answer remains that of forced saving. The answer in the free world should, I believe, be a sustained and imaginative strategy of economic aid by the wealthy to the poor. This we shall discuss later. Here the point need only be stressed that modernization does appear to bring with it a corrective influence on high rates of expansion in the population. If, for instance, in the next twenty years there is a very large increase in the momentum of economic growth in India, there is nothing to suggest that the Japanese rhythm of expansion followed by stabilization may not occur. The basic point remains that without the thrust of growth there is no particular reason why people should want smaller families. Children may die; they cannot be educated; meanwhile they work. A certain fatalism prevails. It is only when hope and expansion begin that the choice of a smaller family makes sense. So the revolution of scientific and capitalist change probably decides the biological revolution as well.

Saving and science are the keys to the revolution of economic growth. Technology is applied science and it results in a great increase in productivity; and productivity is a shorthand way of saying that with the same amount of work we can produce more results, or that we can produce the same results in shorter time and with less effort. Technology, in short, enables us to reinforce the workings of man's hand and brain so that the final output is much greater than could be produced by his own unaided efforts. This, I think, is fairly obvious, and the West has long been a society interested in technology. From the early Middle Ages windmills sailed over the landscape of Western Europe adding the energy of the wind to human efforts.

What is not always so obvious is that technology in all its forms is expensive. The cost of a fully developed technology is formidable. Let us take one example—the building of a large power station to open up a new region to electrification. The preliminaries—levelling the site, constructing roads to it, putting in possibly a branch line to bring in fuel, assembling materials, machines, and generators—are all expensive. Then follows the costly construction period. But if the electricity is to have its full effect, the consequences are more expensive still. Power-lines have to be built, consumer industries developed, trade schools are needed to train both electricians and skilled workers for the new factories. The magnet of more work draws in migrant workers needing housing and urban services. And so it goes on, every step swallowing up capital and setting in motion new demands for still more capital. In other words, if technology is the key to producing more output with less use of resources—productivity—then capital—or saving —is the only key to technology. Without saving, there is no economic growth. Moreover, as we have already remarked, the saving has to be on a fairly massive scale. Under Western colonial control, the poorer countries did see the beginnings of technology—the first roads and ports, some light industries, some development of production for export, a start in education; but the capital involved was not enough to change the whole nature of the economy.

To return to our economic rule of thumb—that when twelve to fifteen per cent of the national income is being devoted to saving, to capital formation, the economy grows—it is important to grasp that the reason for such a percentage is not simply that it allows a country to keep ahead of its growth of population and to set more aside each year for saving; it is also that without a certain momentum of saving, development can remain patchy and the growth of each sector fails to assist the growth of all the rest, railways helping the ports, the ports helping the growing cities, the cities promoting markets for the farms, and factories providing external economies to each other. When the spiral of growth runs right through the economy it begins to be within sight of the break-through to sustained growth. But if capital formation remains below the level needed to create a sort of contagion of development, the result is what you see throughout the developing world where small segments of modernization coexist with stagnant traditional areas and no full momentum of growth develops. So the problem in the first instance is how to achieve the accelerated rate of savings which will ensure a break-through to sustained growth.

Where is the massive injection of capital to come from? We have to remember that developing countries

are, by definition, poor. The process of saving, therefore, will be rugged. Under any conditions, it is very
difficult to make the man who is living on the margin of
subsistence see that only by consuming less now can he
in the future consume more. The saving, after all, is
coming out of his work and effort. It is only human to
want that work to result in some fairly immediate satisfactions, especially the satisfaction of actually getting
enough to eat. The first phase of rugged saving may be
mitigated by importing other people's savings from elsewhere. We shall return to that point. But the first re-
liance has to be on domestic saving, however tough the
process may be.

We can say, broadly speaking, that there are two
chief ways in which capital can be coaxed or induced
to leave the circle of consumption and be drawn into
the creation of more capital goods. It can be done by the
operation of private enterprise in which the profits which
are made by enterprise are then available for further
investment. In conditions of reasonably open competition, the entrepreneur who does the best job in satisfying consumers at least cost to himself earns the biggest
margin for further investment in other undertakings;
and he will use his skill to find out the enterprises which,
once again, maximize profits and hence release more
resources for further investment. This was how the first
cycle of development occurred in Britain and it is still
dominant throughout the Western world.

But of course this is not the only method of diverting
resources from consumption to capital development.

In the West as in the East, the state intervenes by taxation—directly through income taxes, indirectly through sales taxes, and so forth. And where public corporations make profits, then, again indirectly, the state can withdraw resources from consumption and devote them to more capital development. Sales taxes and public profits are the main sources of capital in Soviet Russia.

At this point one limiting factor in the effectiveness of *local* capital should perhaps be mentioned. Quite obviously, local savings are in local currency. They do not automatically buy goods in other lands. Yet just because developing countries are still poor and still lack so much of the technology that they need, they have to find means of bringing in goods and services from abroad; otherwise, they will quite simply not be available. It is for this reason that nearly every break-through to sustained growth has been linked either with the import of capital from abroad or the creation of an export industry which could secure foreign exchange by its sales abroad. The Swedes, for example, sold their lumber overseas and bought the technology of the more developed nations. American growth received a boost from railway-building financed by British capital.

But what happens when the countries have few effective lines of export? When they have few openings for foreign investment or do not command a great deal of confidence in the minds of foreign investors? These are frequent conditions in developing countries. In India, for instance, any increase in national exports will be very arduous. Political insecurity unsettles investment in large parts of Africa. We will return later to this problem when we consider what the wealthy nations might be able to do in the way of a sustained strategy for boosting the revolution of economic growth in poorer countries. Here it is only necessary to underline the point that developing nations not only need capital, they also need a particular kind of capital—foreign exchange.

At this stage of development among the poorer communities it is virtually certain that the state will play a major part in raising more capital for development. This is because in these early days of growth, a large, confident business class is simply not available. Few countries had the long years of merchant dominance such as evolved in Western Europe. Only North America, Australia, and New Zealand began from scratch in a post-feudal age. Everywhere else, leadership has not been with the merchants but with courtiers and landlords—neither of them entrepreneurial types. Even in a country like Japan, which is now what we would call a free-enterprise country, government, not private interests, set in motion all the major industrial projects of the first break-through. Only later were these sold back to the clans and the merchants. By then, they were already going concerns. Throughout most of Africa today, you can count the number of effective African business men on two hands. In parts of Latin America, business has still to disentangle itself from feudal links and limitations. Clearly an almost non-existent entrepreneurial class can hardly launch the revolution of sustained growth. The men are quite simply not there to do it. This is the primary reason why we find a much greater emphasis upon government activity in raising the necessary savings today. In addition, one has to remember the political factor that the accumulation of large profits by a small group of business men is not popular in our modern days of social equality, and there is, therefore, a fairly widespread inhibition against relying massively upon private enterprise.

The more likely pattern is of a good deal of state initiative in the primary stages of growth. However, such a trend does not rule out vigorous private enterprise as well. On the contrary, one of the discoveries of our Western 'mixed economy' in recent years has been the degree to which well planned programs of public investment act as a stimulus to private enterprise. The Monnet Plan remade the base of the French economy and sparked a quite new spirit of recovery in France's private sector. And it, in turn, was launched as a result of the Marshall Plan which, beginning with generous American public grants to Europe, ended by remaking the whole pattern of a dynamic market economy in Western Europe.

A similar process is at work in India today where the very large programs of public investment under the Plans—combined with very strict control over imports —has given Indian private enterprise the best decade in its history. This is not to say that friction and uneasiness between the public and private sectors do not persist. But it is growing less; and there appears to be more comprehension as each side gains in experience and self-confidence.

When it comes to the exact proportions between public and private enterprise, the problem cannot be solved by any rule of thumb; and—except by the Communists —it cannot be solved by any dogmatic statement either. In every country the mix between public and private enterprise is likely to be different, because it will in each case reflect local political pressures, local opportunities, the local scale of developed private enterprise, and the capacity of the country itself to find resources within its own borders. Given such varying opportunities and pre-conditions, it is quite impossible to make an absolute rule, once one leaves behind the ideology of total state control. There is, of course, the opposite ideology of total private enterprise. But this exists nowhere.

The fluctuating role of public and private enterprise does not end the uncertainties. All economics is a matter of choice—of allocating scarce resources to alternative and competing needs. There would be no economics if there were no scarcities. If everything were as available as the air around us or the sky above us, then 'the gloomy science' would not exist. Choice must enter in because there is not enough to go round. And in this field of development it is very easy to make the wrong choices— choices which, in spite of a vast expenditure of money, do not lead to sustained growth, to an upward spiral of interdependent expansion. Getting the 'mix' right is the great factual problem of economic development, and it must vary from economy to economy according to local conditions and endowment.

(101)

However, experience suggests some general points. One can say, for instance, that in our day most of the 'infra-structure'—that is the preliminary capital overheads needed for growth—will be provided in the main by government. Everywhere, the state finances a very large part of the essential investment in human capital —in other words, in education. Transport systems are not often financed by private enterprise these days because returns on them are low and it takes a long time to recover the initial investment. Large power projects also tend to belong, these days, to the public sector. I think one can go further and say that this is a field in which the government's competence to plan and act effectively is fairly widely recognized. To give only one instance: it is very difficult to plan to have too much electric power because the experience of developing economies is that they always need more than they can get. But, of course, some aspects of 'infra-structure' create special economic problems. Housing and schooling do not give a quick return in economic terms, essential as they may be. Their contribution to the economy in better skills, health, and habits of work takes time to mature. Meanwhile, if too much current capital has gone into such social services, government may find itself with no money left to finance immediate-income earners in other fields. It is a difficult question of balance, and false calculations are all too easy.

Government also tends to be more active these days in the field of heavy industry. This was formerly the preserve, in the West, of private enterprise, though government backing and even government subsidies have often played a part in building and sustaining this sector. The reasons for government intervention these days are partly economic, partly political. In developing countries, there may not be entrepreneurs with the confidence or capital to put up a whole steel works; moreover, many new governments are unwilling to entrust anything as crucial and influential as heavy industry entirely to private enterprise. 'The commanding heights of the economy' should, as the Indians argue, be under public control. The result in India has been the creation of a very large public steel industry combined with a doubling in the capacity of private steel-making.

One consequence of sheer scale in this sector is that if errors of calculation are made they tend to be very costly. One of the causes of the wide-spread unrest in Eastern Europe in 1956 was the misplanning of resources in the first days of Communist euphoria. Heavy industry was lavishly planned, and then the units were found to be without adequate raw materials and hence with little hope of economic production. Half-finished steel-mills were symbols of planning that had miscalculated in the most expensive way. The recent cancelling of a whole aircraft industry in East Germany offers another example of costly misplanning. It is said of Mayor LaGuardia that he once said: 'I make very few mistakes, but when I do make a mistake, it's a beaut.' I think you can say that the same is true of governments. They do not necessarily make mistakes in the development of heavy industry. But if they do make a mistake, it tends to be a very large one—in short, a 'beaut.'

In the rest of the industrial structure where scale and need vary enormously, there is a strong case for the effectiveness of private enterprise simply because of the variety of demand and the differences in size of enterprise appropriate to various forms of output. Where consumer demand is highly unpredictable and the need for flexibility in the product is highest, very large industrial organizations are not necessarily the most efficient. To give only one instance, a large bureaucracy is not likely to plan successfully the infinite varieties of feminine clothes. May there not be some inner fatality underlying the fact that, at present, countries of total state control do appear to be singularly ill-dressed?

The desirability of widespread and diversified enterprise does not, however, answer the question whether there are enough entrepreneurs to undertake the expansion. And where they are lacking, as in large parts of Africa, government must inescapably play a part in helping the entrepreneur to begin. Small-scale private enterprise will have to be fostered carefully. This is in part a matter of loans from government and the establishment of properly equipped trading facilities. But perhaps even more important is training in managerial techniques and accountancy. Industrial extension services can in fact be even more important than finance, especially if the finance is not properly supervised. The effort is well worth while. Widespread entrepreneurial talent is one of the most effective forces in the production of greater wealth. In Kenya, for instance, where resources are certainly lower than in some other African countries—say Ghana—the presence of European and Asian business men has given the country a much more rapid rate of industrial growth. But private enterprise cannot grow without encouragement in countries where hitherto the entrepreneurial tradition has been lacking.

This shortage explains why developing countries are anxious that foreign firms should come in to invest, and to establish the new entrepreneurial patterns. In fact, pace-setting private industry can be a valuable legacy of the colonial period. But the legacy gives its full effect only if the foreign companies draw local interests into partnership, encouraging local stockholders to invest, and training local managers and technicians. This has not always been done in the past and this is one reason why foreign enterprise in newly independent countries is often unpopular and governments are torn between the desire to encourage more foreign investment and the fear of having too much.

Now we must turn to what is in some ways the most crucial and difficult problem of all: the transformation of agriculture. Farming, I think, has been the Cinderella of developing economies. So much emphasis has been placed upon the new techniques of industry that it is sometimes forgotten that if farming cannot be transformed there can be no genuine revolution of economic growth. The first reason is that most of the capital has to come from the countryside, because the bulk of the population lives on the land and the bulk of the wealth comes from agriculture in the early days. If farm productivity goes up, a surplus can be transferred to other growing sectors and the farmer will still be better off than he was. This gives him an incentive to produce more food. Prosperity also enables the farming population to provide a growing market for industrial goods. If the countryside is stagnant, the farmers cannot buy the new goods and the beneficent cycle of interdependent upward growth in both industry and agriculture cannot go forward. If you do not change agriculture, you will not change the economy: this is, I think, one of the safe rules one can lay down for developing communities. At the same time, agriculture is the most difficult sector to change for the simple reason that agricultural methods are thousands of years old and people prefer on the whole to go on in the ways of their fathers. To coax the traditional farmer still at work in his old setting into new patterns of agriculture is infinitely more difficult than to persuade people to undertake new techniques in a wholly new, industrial urban environment. In the city, all is new; change is part of the landscape. On the land, everything seems the same; this makes change so much more difficult.

To transform farming solely by means of private enterprise offers some formidable difficulties. The chief instrument of change is the development of the market, the incentive to production which market prices offer. But will the farmers come into the market? Private landowners in under-developed areas are very rarely enterprising. Whether it is a question of the Zamindars in India, the tribal leaders of Africa, or the feudal land-

(106)

lords of Latin America, they are not, as a group, intent on transforming their lands and their techniques. They still live for subsistence and display. The peasants have no incentive to change since any gain could go to swell the landlord's rent. Tribal farmers face comparable inhibitions because sharing the fruits of work with the clan discourages intensive effort.

The first answer to these obstacles is, of course, ambitious land reform. The peasant must own his land. Where he does not, modernization is unlikely. But this does not end the problem. In many lands, the pressure of population is such that no farmer can receive an effective economic unit once the land has been split up. Uneconomic, fragmented holdings push production further down. Once again, there is an answer; but it is not a cheap or easy one. A massive development of co-operative societies for credit, processing, and marketing can give the small farmer the advantages of scale and the inducements of private ownership. This has been done triumphantly in Japan where a five-acre farm can give a decent living because it is backed by co-operatives organized and run by the farmers themselves. But such a development takes time, patience, and a great deal of capital.

I doubt, however, whether there are any short cuts. It is very tempting for the state to believe that there are: collectivize the land, employ the peasants as so many day-labourers, and in this way repeat in agriculture what is in fact the basic pattern in industry. But agriculture is not industry. Peasants in developing countries feel for their land and for their beasts and for the rhythms and satisfactions of their farming life in ways which are quite different from the reactions of men to machines and factories. The mood may change, of course. Western farmers increasingly regard farming as simply a business. But the need to change agriculture is not a future problem. It is urgent and immediate. If the state steps in too aggressively, the result seems to be a profound underground opposition to the whole idea of transforming agriculture under state direction. Even after forty years, Russian agriculture is still the chief trouble-spot of the régime. In China, the desperate move of transforming the whole of agriculture according to a communal system—in which in essence people work on the industrial pattern—has, at least in some measure, broken down as a result of the peasants' resistance and apathy. In fact, no state-run agriculture today reflects anything like the productivity of Japanese or American agriculture. In Yugoslavia, where output is going up most sharply among public systems of farming, the emphasis is heavily on decentralization and workers' control. Perhaps the failure can best be illustrated by a remark made at an agronomists' conference held a short time ago at Bangalore. Agricultural scientists had gathered there from all over the world. At the end of the discussion, the Yugoslav delegate was asked to sum up. This is what he said: 'There are two main agricultural problems in the world: American agriculture produces too much; Russian agriculture produces too little. But we have the solution, gentlemen. If Russia will use American methods and America will use Russian methods, there will be no further problem.' This is perhaps an apt summary of the degree to which massive state intervention in agriculture has so far failed to produce results.

And yet the problem remains. The transformation of agriculture cannot be secured without massive investment. In fact, one reason for the Russian effort to enlarge the scale of farms is to produce economic units substantial enough to absorb large inputs of capital. Yet the capital must also in the early stages come largely from rural savings and be deployed in fierce competition from other driving needs—education, transport, power, industry. In this competition, the tendency has been to overlook the essential demands of farming. In India's Second Plan, for instance, or in Pakistan's First, agricultural priorities were too low. The new Plans correct this bias; for the realization is growing that without capital the land cannot progress. All the methods of transforming agriculture are expensive. Farmers need more skills, more fertilizers, more credit. There is no hope of a productive agriculture if saving is squeezed out of the country and nothing is put back.

Perhaps this is just another way of saying that all the methods of economic transformation are expensive. There are none that can be accomplished without some capital, and many of the most crucial ones demand great sums of capital. The scale of capital raises, therefore, the crucial political problem. Can you persuade people to undertake this degree of saving voluntarily?

May it not be an essential short cut to allow the state to step in and say to the citizen: 'You must save; you will save; and it is good for you even if you object.' Such a short cut is not easy under a democratic government. Voters may will the end of development. They do not relish the means—higher taxes, higher savings. So the question must be asked: does dictatorial government enjoy a built-in advantage in developing lands? At this point, however, the economic problem fuses with the political problem which must be examined next.

Chapter Five

The Politics of Development

THE TIME has now come
to look at the fourth of the great revolutions of our day:
the revolution of political equality. It is everywhere at
work in the under-developed and uncommitted nations
and everywhere, too, it complicates and even exacer-
bates relations between the rich nations and the poor.
It is an all-embracing concept of equality: equality of
the nation, of the race, of the class; above all, the equality
of man with man in the new world-society that is beginning to emerge.

(111)

Most of the poor and uncommitted lands have acquired this vast, almost cosmic vision of equality as a result of their colonial contact with Western societies. The ambition to modernize, to pull level with the more developed societies, has been implanted in them by their experiences as part of a Western imperial pattern. Western merchants, Western educators, Western administrators, brought the ferment of the new ideas and the new sense of the need for, and the right to, equality.

But these Western contacts brought in the new ideas by different routes. There have been positive, constructive, and creative methods of transmission; and the work of great imperial administrators—one thinks of a Monroe or an Elphinstone in India, a Lugard or a Guggisberg in West Africa—undoubtedly created a framework of order and opportunities of advance unequalled for centuries. It is in this sense that empire has proved one of the great civilizing forces in human history. But these were not the only methods by which the sense of equality was fostered. We must not forget the dark ways of dislike, exclusion, fear, and prejudice, which make imperialism one of the catastrophic forces of mankind as well.

During the West's impact on the surrounding world —an impact which has lasted three hundred years— there is evidence enough of both forms of transmission. We have already spoken of the great administrators who laid the foundations upon which such services as the Indian Civil Service came to be not only efficient and selfless, but even a nation-building force. Today, with the collapse of the Congo before us, we are less likely to underestimate the supreme contribution orderly administration can make to the arts of civilization.

To the administrators we must add the missionaries and the scholars. Not all missionaries came out in the spirit in which fruitful cultural contact can flourish. Too much contempt for the 'heathen,' too much ignorance of alien cultures diminished the effectiveness of what was done. Had more gone with the sympathy and understanding displayed by Father Matteo Ricci, the great Jesuit missionary to China, who knows what new insights might not have been achieved? Yet the influence of Christianity on great Indian reformers such as Sir Ram Mohan Roy or great leaders like Gandhi should not be forgotten. In Africa, the figure of David Livingstone, working with fortitude to end the slave-trade, towers above the greedy mob of adventurers and profiteers looking to Africa, like Pistol, for its 'golden joys.' And throughout West Africa, unknown heroes of the Protestant missions risked almost certain death by yellow fever to bring religion, education, and the first beginnings of modern health to the Africans. Nor should one forget the work of Western scholars who have played so great a role in piecing together from the records of monuments, temple scrolls, and archaeology the history of Asian peoples who might otherwise have lost their history, and their identity as well.

Another essential element in a developing society— a modern managerial class—was also introduced through the Western impact. There would have been no quick development of a modern middle class with effective commercial and entrepreneurial energies if colonial rule had not created a new atmosphere of peace and fostered, in great countries such as India, the development of modern commercial law, the notion of contract, a new sense of security for property, a new belief that if the merchant sets to work to develop, accumulate, and invest, his wealth should be secure.

Nor is the role of the army negligible. Elements of discipline and service were injected into traditional communities as a result of modern army training. In fact, one could argue that in some countries the officer corps had qualities of loyalty and patriotism free from any tincture of self-interest not found too generally in the community at large. To have such cadres is a positive achievement upon which much can be built.

Yet it would be a grave mistake if we in the West thought only of the constructive efforts and forgot the darker side of the record. Take first of all the most resented aspect of Western rule, particularly of British rule: we took with us in our colonial dealings an ignorant and almost irremovable racial prejudice. Now I know that most nations have had their racial prejudices; in fact, I am reminded of a Chinese proverb to the effect that God first made the African and overbaked him black, and then God made the European and underbaked him white, but then God made the Chinese and baked them exactly right—which is yellow of course. And it is an irony of history that in the nineteenth century, the Chinese called Westerners 'red' barbarians; perhaps because there were so many Scotsmen among them. Prejudice, the sense of separateness and superiority, are certainly not confined to the West.

But for three hundred years the white race has enjoyed a dominant position in the world. Its members were able to stamp their prejudices across the face of the globe because they were, in fact, on top. And there can be no doubt that many white men, particularly Anglo-Saxon white men, cannot overcome a straightforward colour prejudice. And this belief that coloured people are inferior has left its mark all over the world. Perhaps one realizes how deep the wounds are only when one has lived in ex-colonial lands. Occasionally in confidential talks, late at night, when there is no longer an official front to be kept up, one hears of the insults at the hands of London boarding-house keepers or of careless wounding words from educated people: trivial incidents, perhaps, but ones which leave a mark on people's consciousness that can never be effaced.

Another whole set of problems is concerned not so much with race as with class. It seems to be a fact of life that in the early days of industrial development, the merchant, in process of turning himself into an entrepreneur, often demonstrates facets of greed and rapacity which make him a not too attractive figure to the society he raids and exploits. This of course is not a problem confined to the newly developing areas. If you read the pages of Dickens, you will meet the Mr. Merdles and the Mr. Veneerings who pursue wealth with a passion and irresponsibility that leads them to ruin others and finally themselves. Yet such men are influential. Money

talks. And in a poor but developing economy it is much
more likely that such men will have contacts with the
colonial rulers, be consulted by them, and entertain
them. There is probably no very great identification of
interests. British colonial administrators tended to
think of business men as the Victorians thought of trade.
It was not quite 'the thing.' But there was enough contact to create some identification between colonial rule
and the local magnates, and to give a social edge to
nationalist criticism.

It was reinforced wherever—as was usual—the landlord system remained intact. The administrators arriv-
ing from overseas to take up their imperial appointments
would not refuse the offered tiger-hunt. Again, some
identification was possible between colonial rule and
the local social hierarchy.

The educated groups in the new sense—the new
lawyers, the new technicians, the men and women who
had access to modern forms of knowledge—remained a
very small group in relation to the people at large. A
sense of isolation tended to weaken them and undermine
their political confidence. Moreover, the environment
confused them further. After a number of small hopeful
beginnings, colonial economies failed to move forward
to sustained momentum. The economic picture was
patchy, with bits of development here and bits of development there, while social changes went forward in
one sector and were quite absent in others. Young
people had the feeling of belonging to a discontinuous
society—a mood which increased their unease. And to

all this we must add the stagnation of the twenties and the thirties.

After the First World War, the colonial powers of Western Europe entered upon a period of relative economic decline. It was followed by the appalling depression of 1929 and the chaotic conditions of the thirties. Local stagnation increased the social discontents of the colonial world and coupled rising political consciousness with social protest and economic frustration. It was no longer only the tiny educated middle class who felt the pressure. More unsophisticated people began to ask questions about the foreigner who came and lived in the big house at the top of the hill, the colonial officials with all the influential administrative jobs, the big foreign merchant and banker with something of an economic monopoly. And round these foreigners tended to cluster the few members of the local society who were doing well out of the system: the large landowner, the local merchant, the new industrialist whose wealth—old or new—cut them off more and more from their frustrated fellow countrymen.

It is therefore not surprising that the revolution of independence and national equality which has been gathering strength round the world for the last fifty years has more than one political and social overtone. There is the ambition for economic change sparked by the example of what Western society can do with its new technology. To it must be added the social unrest stirred up by the contrast between the small rich *élite,* comfortably profiting from the *status quo,* and the vast mass of the people who are beginning to resent their desperate poverty. This, in turn, fuses with anti-colonial sentiment, with the feeling that the subject nation has the right to self-government and independence. In fact, the two are often barely distinguishable; for local opinion tends more and more to see 'colonial servitude' as the chief obstacle to social rights and economic development. These were the days when students like Chou En-lai or Ho Chi-minh went to Europe for their education and found that only Leninism really seemed to describe their predicament. A stirring, uncertain, chaotic time of social, political, and economic change, all woven together—this, I think, is how we must regard the struggle of the poorer nations to get through all the sound-barriers of their life at once: the economic barrier, the social barrier, the political barrier. And if one sees the struggle in this perspective, surely it is not surprising that our days are tense. The remarkable thing is how much stability still remains in the midst of these whirling passions and ambitions for total change.

At one time, it must have seemed that the whole colonial order, battered by such pressures, would end in a violent explosion of hatred and violence. Some experiments have ended in bloodshed. The Dutch left Indonesia after war had decided the issue. The French withdrew from Indo-China under the same tragic star of conflict. Britain had to fight an ugly little war in Cyprus before a settlement could be reached. Certainly Lenin foresaw such a consummation and even suggested that the revolt of the colonial masses might be a quicker route to world Communism than the milder resentments of Western workers.

But in fact, the transfer of power from the old colonial governments to the new independent states since the war has, I think, proved easier than we might have feared. We can now see that, at least in these first decades of independence, the transfer of power by Britain to India and Pakistan—the first great voluntary transfers of government—was accomplished with such restraint and generosity that a new pattern of compelling force appeared on the human scene. It was, of course, an achievement towards which British political thought had long been directed. As early as the eighteen-twenties, great British proconsuls in India had said that there could be no justification for British rule in India save to build up the conditions under which Indians would govern themselves. The evolving Commonwealth in which the white Dominions—Canada, Australia—had already found an independent place provided a structure of friendship and co-operation within which the new nations could fit without any diminution of their newly established sovereignty. But equally, the transfer was made possible by the political vision and immense personal generosity of men like Gandhi and Nehru who were ready, when the day came, to treat their former gaolers as trusted friends. For this mutual respect and conciliation there was no place in the Marxist canon, and it has had a dominant influence ever since.

Transfers of power have continued to take place with similar grace and dignity in other parts of the world—

in the rest of the British Commonwealth, in French West Africa. In fact, one can say that there are perhaps only two types of ex-colonial community in which it is excessively difficult to achieve a transfer of power with anything like the goodwill that is needed to make it effective and peaceful. One type is the country where a settler problem complicates the issue—as in Algeria, in the Rhodesias, or in Kenya. In such communities, the lines of cleavage between groups—the political, social, and economic lines we have already discussed—are strengthened and exacerbated by the greatest dividers of all, the dividers of culture and race. Settlers from the metropolitan country come in and root themselves in the local community. They take the best land. Being better educated, they produce more wealth from it. They hold the best posts. They often control the administration. At the same time, internal peace and the beginnings of modernization can set in motion a violent explosion of the birth-rate among the more primitive peoples whose chief means of subsistence—the land— has nonetheless been taken away. Two societies develop. In one, the white settlers build up a more or less wealthy modern community. Around and among them the dispossessed exist, multiply, and finally begin to revolt. This has been the pattern of Algeria. In Kenya, in the Rhodesias, in parts of the Congo, acute racial differences complete the picture of separatism and hostility. Here the transfer of power presents overwhelming difficulty. The long bitter Algerian war is testimony to the vast obstacles that must be overcome.

The second category is rather more ambiguous. In some countries the transfer of power is made, but conditions prevent it from convincing the local people that a genuine transfer has in fact occurred. Lenin had these cases in mind when he argued that metropolitan powers could still exercise a preponderant influence in ex-colonial territories, simply by keeping all the levers of economic power in their own hands. Any form of foreign investment, particularly investment from a dominant Western or ex-imperial government, had hidden in it, he suggested, the tentacles of continued control. One cannot underestimate the degree to which the Leninist myth of power by indirection, exercised through 'the monopolists and the trusts,' has sunk into the distrustful minds of developing peoples. Where in fact investment from abroad seems overwhelmingly dominant and the doubt can arise whether local interests have any chance against the big foreign firms, then the Leninist pattern is not too difficult to apply and people begin to ask whether their own supposedly independent government may not be the puppet of a foreign power. There was an element of this feeling in the Cuban reaction to Batista; and we do not yet know what sorrows have been brought upon the Congo by the decision of a separatist government to establish itself in the Katanga where Belgian mining interests are overwhelmingly strong.

Yet we are now realizing for the first time that, in spite of these difficulties, it is not in fact the moment of transfer of power that is most difficult in the emergence of the poorer nations to a sense of national

equality in the modern world. After all, in the periods
that lead up to the ending of the colonial régime, usually
a considerable sense of common purpose unites the
country. More and more people come to feel that colonial rule must be the chief target and that all differences
of race or tribe or class can be subordinated to the
greater struggle to achieve political equality and independence. This is the great unifying force behind
such movements as India's Congress Party where the
rich mill-owner and the simple peasant hand-weaver
were united under the leadership of Gandhi and Nehru.
This unifying force is enough to carry the country forward to the great effort of achieving independence. In
fact, the greater the effort, the greater the unity. Where
independence comes virtually without struggle—as in
Burma or Ceylon or Nigeria—the advantages of national
unity may well be lessened. It is after independence
that the real troubles begin. With national equality and
independence achieved, the problems of social and
economic equality begin to take pride of place.

The first and obvious conflict to gather force is the
fundamental conflict between rich and poor within the
nation. Gone is the overriding unity of struggle. The
contrasts between wealth and poverty are now all the
more stark because, during the struggle, independence
had been painted in millennial terms, with milk and
honey for everybody.

If, as often happens, independence coincides with
the early days of industrialization and economic modernization, then the conflict may take on even sharper

social overtones. At this period the merchant-turned-en-
trepreneur is not necessarily an inspiring national
leader, not often a man to whom the masses will turn
with a sense that his integrity is unquestioned and his
work unequivocally for the public good. A lot of the
prejudice one meets in India—for example, against the
Mawari trading-class—is based on the fact that the
masses believe, not always without foundation, that
these men will put profit before everything, even before
the well-being of the community. The belief breeds acri-
mony, distrust, and class-hatred.

The new entrepreneur is an object of suspicion because he gets on too fast. Another dominant group—
the landlords—are often disliked for the opposite reason: they do not change themselves and thus make
change impossible for everyone else on the land. They
are still so embedded in the past, still so set upon the
old questions of status, the old attitude towards land
as a way of life not as a way of development, that often
it seems as though an immovable social and political
lid had been clapped tightly down on the countryside,
inhibiting any possibility of development and change.
The unhandiness of unchanged feudal leadership for
a modernizing economy can be illustrated from Japan
after 1870 where the Meiji reformers found it necessary
to begin their economic revolution by total land reform.
In many parts of Latin-America today, land reform is
probably still the single most efficacious way of setting
in motion the processes of economic growth.

The shortcomings of leadership based upon the old

rural leaders and the up-and-coming entrepreneurs of the city are not overcome simply by introducing the formal machinery of parliamentary democracy. All too often, the present groups in power simply manipulate the democratic machine for their own purposes. They resemble in some measure the House of Commons in Britain before 1832 when the landed gentry had the margin of political strength. But Britain's parliamentary government became an efficacious instrument of social change only after several further modifications. It was widened first to include the rising middle classes including, of course, the entrepreneurs and then later, after a very considerable advance in literacy, the mass of the citizens as well.

These pre-conditions of parliamentary effectiveness often do not exist in developing economies on the morrow of independence. The entrepreneurial groups are still socially irresponsible; there are no Lord Shaftesburys, no Disraelis to express the conscience of the dominant class. In addition, the middle class is miserably small and has none of the self-confidence of the bustling Victorian world. And the mass of the people are wholly illiterate and are still overwhelmingly country folk at the mercy of local lords or bailiffs or, as in much of Africa, unaware of any leadership or change outside the tribal pattern. In such conditions the machinery of democracy is not enough to create its spirit. Parliament tends to remain an affair of cliques and manipulators. Pakistan before Ayub, Iran, the Egypt of Farouk—all are examples of systems, which though parliamentary in form, were and are in fact self-regarding, oligarchic, and to a considerable degree anti-social.

Since the old rural leaders and the new rich are so often unable to canalize the new ambitions of the people, they are often thrust aside in the years following independence. Again and again it is the army that steps in to provide new government: in the Sudan, in Egypt, in Iraq, in Pakistain. The representatives of the merchant and landlord groups are set aside, and military leaders, coming in with a tradition of service and a reputation of integrity, take over and attempt to pull the country together to face the truly daunting problems of development in the first stages of independence.

And I think we would do well to remember how daunting these problems are. The first and deepest is the dilemma we have already explored. In early days of economic development, there is no hope for expansion unless the people can be persuaded to undertake a large and expanding program of capital saving. Yet they are poor—poor by definition since the wealth-creating process has yet to begin. Saving for them entails lopping off a margin from current consumption when consumption is already so low that it is barely enough to sustain life. Even though the hope is that, five and ten years from now, conditions will be better, can the people be persuaded—least of all by free vote —to submit themselves to an even worse plight now? The dilemma, as we have seen, is absolutely inescapable because the need for saving is as unavoidable as the fact of poverty. It needs exceptional leadership, with very considerable administrative capacity and imaginative grasp, to ease the people out of this particular trap; and these qualities are not easily forthcoming in the traditional groups who make up the leadership in transitional societies.

The problem is made all the more involved by the fact that the coming of independence is precisely the hour when the hopes of the people are most acutely roused by the possibilities of achieving a modern form of society. The colonial struggle gave them political consciousness. They were told again and again during its course that only the wicked imperialists hold them back from a better life. Thus, when independence comes, they expect that better life and they expect it now. It is against this background that we should assess the pressures on their leaders.

To maintain themselves in power—the first commandment for politicians—they must be able to meet some of this rising popular pressure and to show some positive results. The chances are, however, that the turmoil of transition has lessened administrative efficiency, weakened disciplines of work, and possibly slowed down the entry of foreign capital. Economic conditions may well be worse. The pressures mount all the more rapidly as a result. These pressures are much greater than our stabler, wealthier world now finds easy to imagine. The only striking analogy that comes to mind is the pressure on any Western government if unemployment rises above a certain level. But to gauge the force of protest and discontent in the developing

(126)

countries one would need to multiply the pressure a thousandfold. The issue is not simply one of being out of work for a time; it is all future possibility of work, all hope of a little wealth to come, the whole chance of moving on from stagnation and misery. Such pressure is political dynamite.

These conditions alone would be enough to tax the powers of leadership in the new state to the full and even to make the new rulers feel that they must take dictatorial powers in order to find the direction and discipline needed to face the nation's inescapable problems. But in addition to all these internal problems, they face an even more testing external difficulty. They have all come to power during the bitter international tensions of the Cold War.

They can neither change nor modify the broad struggle for power in the world in which the Great Powers maneuver to maintain their position, to extend their dominion and to achieve predominant influence. Smaller states may be able to play a part at the margin and, unhappily, as the pre-1914 crises in the Balkans showed, shifts of power at the margin can precipitate the general struggle. But the core of the fight is not theirs to influence. Dr. Nkrumah is never tired of quoting an old Swahili proverb which says that when the bull elephants fight, the grass is trampled down. In many parts of the world, the sense that the poorer, weaker nations are pawns in a bigger game, just grass to be trodden down in the struggle by the great ones, lends a tragic and, I think, moving edge to the search for neutralism. In the past, the Western Powers have often shown too little sympathetic understanding for the mood. The United States for years under the late Mr. John Foster Dulles condemned neutralism as a moral evil, forgetting its own early distaste for 'entangling alliances.' But the 'morals' of resistance for very small states in the age of the fifty megaton bomb are at least dubious and it is not certain, in any case, whether a neutrality prepared to defend itself is not a much better safeguard than co-operation in alliances with the West.

The reason is very simple. Mass opinion still tends to become very easily anti-Western because colonial memories are so recent. To build alliances with the ex-colonial powers can easily be twisted to look like falling once again under their imperial control. This twist, it need hardly be said, is staple Communist propaganda. The royal government in Iraq fell in part because of its readiness to work with the West in a Middle-Eastern military alliance.

The blame is not all on one side. Neutralists have also earned suspicion by the way in which they have interpreted neutrality. Unfortunately the Cold War not only scares smaller powers; it also offers them temptations which very often they are unable to resist. It is, after all, very tempting for a local leader to think that he can play the Great-Power game. It gives a great sense of importance to believe himself able to play off America against Russia. The advantages at first seem greater than the risks. That by riding the tiger one may end up inside is not too obvious in the early stages of the game. If, for instance, you are having trouble with the opposition, why not turn to the Communists and get a little help? The problem of getting the Communists to *stop* helping afterwards belongs to a future too distant to be taken into account. In other words, the danger offered to small governments is not only a direct risk of invasion or attack but also a permanent temptation to involve themselves far out of their depth in the rapids and shoals of world politics.

I do not myself think we should meet this situation by succumbing to irritation and denunciation. It is tempting to lose one's patience and exclaim against local leaders who seem so irresponsible. But could we not try sometimes to put ourselves in their position? Are they not like adolescents who leave their father's house only to be involved instantly in an enormous street fight; or like children who go out into the great school of the world only to find the professors shooting it out in just those classrooms where they had hoped to get their education? One cannot, I think, underline too much the inexperience and the sense of uncertainty which must prevail among new leaders who enter the school of the world and find the faculty throwing everything, including their desks, at each other. I confess that my own feeling is not one of irritation but rather of intense sympathy for leaders who have to take the first steps of independence over ground which gives way at every step.

However, there is no escape from the fact that for

the time being the Cold War forms the environment of the modern world. The Communists' attempt at world dominion is one of the great ideological strains in their faith; however much their tactics may vary, the underlying strategy has not yet changed. Equally, the Western powers will not abandon their desire to preserve a world in which plurality of power and capacity for choice are possible. The two aims are not compatible and all along the frontiers of the two worlds the struggle for influence and dominance cannot be evaded. We have therefore to assess the impact of the Cold War on the problems of developing states and to see how the rival ideologies influence local aspirations, particularly the great central driving aspiration to equal status and an equal chance.

We would, I think, be unwise to underestimate some of the immediate advantages which the Communists enjoy in this tough tussle for influence in the newly independent nations. For one thing, this is a time of chaotic change and hence of chaotic ideas. It is dangerously attractive to many minds to be offered a political and economic panacea as complete and apparently self-explanatory as Marxism-Leninism. It seems to tie up all their problems in a single order of explanation and to make sense of a world which they feel they do not understand and fear they never may. Another advantage enjoyed by Communism is that in Asia, in Africa, in Latin America, Russia does not bear the stigma of having been a colonial power. This is paradoxical when you consider how much of Central Asia's non-Russian peoples are under Soviet control. But Russia's extension across Central Asia and Siberia to embrace so many Turkoman and Mongol peoples within its empire has the same irresistible, irreversible, almost geological force as China's imperial extension southwards or the engulfing of most of North America by the United States.

Moreover, the subject peoples—Kazakhs, Kirghiz, Uzbeks—have been drawn into the advantages of modern society as well as into its pains. The nomads from the steppes were thrown into the modernizing, industrializing process as ruthlessly as the Bantu of South Africa have been flung into the mines. But today such educational advance has accompanied the process that there are more graduates per head of population in Uzbekistan than in France. The Bantu of the Union of South Africa and the fellaga of Algeria have not fared so well. They have been left on the margins of the new modern society, unintegrated, unreconciled, the sullen proletariat of revolt. Add to this Russia's apparent freedom from racial prejudice, and its advantages in the minds of developing peoples should be clear.

Then there are a number of reasons in practical politics to explain the Communists' advantage. When a new nation is faced with the enormous complexity and variety of economic and social problems that are inescapable after independence, the temptation to impose the rule of a single party and use hard discipline to solve them is obvious. And there stands the Communist Party ready-made, offering its pattern of total obedience.

Nationalist leaders looking for policies in the post-revolutionary phase are caught by the deceptive direction and vigour of the Communist solution.

It can, I think, be argued that this availability of the Soviet pattern helps to explain the unfolding paradox of the Castro régime in Cuba—a régime brought in by widespread popular revolt against the dictatorship and corruption of Batista, promising elections and civil liberties; yet degenerating almost at once into another kind of police state. There is evidence to suggest that Castro chose a Marxist pattern not because he had drawn his support from embattled peasants and workers —in fact, middle-class disgust with Batista was his strongest suit—but because it was the only pattern he knew to help him to exercise the power he had unexpectedly achieved. Faced with the multitudinous uncertainties of responsibility, he grabbed the only pattern which seemed likely to preserve his leadership and deal with his difficulties. It was Cuba's tragedy that a nation so relatively advanced in development—to give only one instance, more than half its population already live in the cities—should be thrust back by totally inexperienced leadership to a repressive and brutal system usually associated with much earlier stages of break-through.

It is, of course, not only a question of Communism offering ready-made solutions. Many of them seem to fit the real dilemmas very closely. At a time when changing the old leadership and bringing the masses into the new dynamic economy are pre-conditions of development, there is no doubt where Communism stands. It is against the old landlord; it is against the new entrepreneur. It sides with the majority of the people whose aspirations are the motive force of change. The content of their policy also has its relevance. The Russians claim that such is their ability to achieve large rates of growth in the last forty years, that they can offer a pattern of rapid development and rapid capital accumulation in just those areas where the countries of the newly independent world most need help. They claim that their scale of capital formation has driven them forward at growth-rates of six, seven, and eight per cent a year, and the massive Communist drive for capital and production will quickly outstrip anything that the West, with its bungling experimental methods, can hope to offer. All this is heady stuff to a young government looking round desperately for policies with which to cope with all the problems of its day, and not perhaps sophisticated enough to grasp what the cost of so much 'discipline' may be.

Nor do the Communists simply leave their claimed achievements to talk for themselves. Propaganda underlines them incessantly and offers of capital assistance reinforce the picture of Soviet success. Again and again missions set off to Moscow from Africa or Asia or Latin America and there receive offers of help in buying up the surpluses the West will not buy and capital assistance at very low rates of interest for a long period of time. At times it is almost as though the projects themselves—an Aswan Dam, a Volta Dam, a steel-mill for

India—had become small sectors in the general fluctuating battle-front of world assistance. The building and the competition are not necessarily bad. On the contrary, more capital may be flowing into the under-developed areas than would otherwise be the case. But the political overtones, the sense of rivalry and pressure with which so much of the aid is beset, adds enormously to the political dilemmas of the poor nations reaching out desperately for a new way of life.

Given this context of competition, what shall we say of Western policies? Before we consider our positive aims and policies, I think we should realize soberly that the world-wide struggle is not necessarily 'going our way,' that we have formidable difficulties to overcome. The fact remains that the Western powers have been the colonial masters until the day before yesterday. Although the grace of making the transfers of imperial power has helped lessen colonial resentments, we still carry the ugly stigma of racialism. We are still implicated in the dangerous problem of apartheid in South Africa. We have our own Deep Souths and Notting Hills. We do not come with clean hands.

Again, the political pattern of multi-party democracy which we prefer, and often set up in colonies before we leave them, is not necessarily workable in the first turbulent days of independence. Crises at these times are not much less rigorous than our own crises of war, and we in the West usually meet such crises with governments of national union. So it is in most ex-colonies. Single-party government represents the clear-cut leadership needed when times are insanely complex and confused. Such government need not be Communist. But it is also unlikely to resemble the West's advanced political democracy. Nor is it simply a matter of crisis. A certain sophistication is also involved. If a leader has spent his life to achieve self-government from the foreigner, he cannot find it easy to give government up five years after independence because some newer leader has appeared on the scene.

Some of our economic patterns are difficult, too. Many Western governments put great emphasis on private investment as a chief instrument of economic development. But this runs into two opposite difficulties. Private capital on the scale needed to achieve 'take-off' would need to be so great that it would arouse nationalist or Leninist suspicions locally—especially if Western companies pushed their customary policy of seeking local participation not very vigorously or not at all.

The opposite difficulty is that, in fact, so much private capital is not usually forthcoming in any case and to rely on it alone would delay development indefinitely.

Of course, this difficulty has in fact been met by the great extension of Western public assistance programs in the last decade—to which the United States has made by far the largest contribution. But two things are clear about public aid. The rest of the free world has made no contribution commensurate with America's or with their own post-Marshall wealth. Certainly few have given anything like the one per cent of national income —which cannot surely be considered an excessive contribution to world development. The second point is that the aid programs have not been part of a general development strategy designed to bring the poor nations to 'take-off' in the shortest time. Capital has been voted year by year in a haphazard way. Trade policies have even pulled in the other direction. There are thus new challenges to face, a new strategy to be worked out, new decisions to be taken.

Of one thing I am certain: if we continue with what is surely our greatest Western temptation, and think that in some way history owes us a solution, that we can, by pursuing our own most parochial self-interest, achieve in some miraculous way a consummation of world order, then we are heading not simply towards great disappointments, but towards disaster and tragedy as well. There has to be a new start, new plans, a new approach. Otherwise we prepare for our defeat simply by default.

Chapter Six

Not by Bread Alone

ALL THE great revolutions of our contemporary world had their origin round the North Atlantic. The revolution by which equality has become a driving force in political life, the new concern with material things, the absorption in scientific analysis, the spurt of growth in the world's population, the whole transformation of our economic system by the application of technology and capital: all these vast changes were launched in the North Atlantic arena. Yet if you look at these Atlantic nations today they make the strange impression of not being particularly concerned with the revolutions they have wrought. The changes have been unleashed on mankind. Blindly,

(137)

blunderingly, with immense impact and immense confusion, they are remaking the face of the earth. But
can one say that the Western powers follow their course
with any intimate concern? Do they see them as direct
projections of the Western way of life or accept responsibility for the fact that it was the Western colonial system that chiefly set in motion the present world-wide
movement of revolutionary change?

Is it not strange to care so little for what we have
launched; to lose interest in our inventions just when
they are beginning to have their maximum impact?
And if one asks why we behave in this way, I suppose
some of the answers are not entirely comfortable. It
seems to be a law of life that when you become rich
you tend to become complacent. What is the Biblical
phrase? 'They sat down to eat and they rose up to play.'
Since the post-war economic revival in the West, the
feeling has become fairly general that things are not
going too badly. Elections have been fought on the
slogan: 'You never had it so good'; great nations have
been lulled with the promise of 'peace and prosperity.'
The once militant working class substitutes 'I'm all
right, Jack' for 'Workers of the world, unite.' This mood
of ease and complacency inevitably limits our ability
to understand the needs and hungers of the millions who
have not yet found their way into the modern world.
To be rich and to be complacent invites the nemesis of
such a condition—which is by indifference and by a
narrowing of the heart to lose contact with the urgent
desires of the great mass of one's fellow men. This con-

striction of pity can happen to individual men and women. History has always shown it. Today perhaps we see a new phenomenon: rich communities succumbing to the same limitation of human understanding.

But there is another more subtle reason that helps to explain why we are not as interested as we might be in all the revolutions we have launched. We simply cannot, out of our own experience, measure their truly daunting difficulties. All of them happened in the Western world under the conditions of maximum convenience. The West was relatively under-populated; it was immensely well endowed with the resources that are needed for the new kind of economy. Iron ore and coal were plentiful for the launching of industry. The great plains of North America and Southern Russia quickly began to pour out food for the new industrial millions.

But perhaps the chief reason for our over-confidence is to be found in the mechanism by which, in the main, the Western break-through to sustained growth was accomplished. In the critical early stages of change, the profit motive proved to be an immensely powerful engine of growth. Its success implanted deeply in the minds of many of us the idea that the greatest good of the greatest number can be achieved provided each individual or company or even nation vigorously pursues its own self-interest. The strength of the case lies in the fact that, up to a point and under certain conditions, the premise may well be right. Competition in a free market has produced enormous gains in wealth and efficiency. In fact, we are living today through another such burst of growth as the tariff barriers go down inside the Common Market. But equally the conditions in Western Europe between the wars showed that if each nation pursued its own self-interest by a wrong route—in this case by constantly increasing its protective tariffs—the end result was not the good of all but the ruin of each. Nor has the Common Market come about by the unguided pressure of local interests. On the contrary, it has been an act of high statesmanship, pursued by dedicated political leaders and purposefully formulated by planners associated with M. Jean Monnet —surely one of the most quietly and effectively revolutionary groups the world has ever known.

In other words, there are conditions in which the unchecked pursuit of self-interest is an excellent guide to socially desirable action. There are also conditions when it is not. But the West still has a certain bias towards believing in its general efficacy, without regard to the framework within which it is to act. We tend to have a Micawberish attitude towards life, a feeling that so long as we do not get too excited something is certain to turn up. Yet if we look back over history I do not think the experience of other generations teaches us precisely this lesson. On the contrary, it suggests that not the Micawbers, but those who will, and want, and work, are more likely to see their plans and visions realized. It is, therefore, a disturbing reflection that in our own day the amount of effort, interest, preparation, and sheer slogging hard work which the Communists tend to put into the task of building *their* version of world order very greatly exceeds what we are ready to do or the sacrifices we are prepared to make. Even more obviously, their vision of a world brotherhood made one by Communism outstrips the scale of our imagination. The West thinks only marginally in terms of the whole world, the whole family of man. Each group tends to concentrate on its own parochial interests. There is apparently no energy comparable to the world-wide ambitions that set the Communists to work from one end of our planet to the other.

If we are to face the vast gap between the rich nations and the poor, between the nations round the Atlantic area which have been through their modernizing revolutions and the searching nations all around the world who seek desperately to make the same transition, perhaps the first decision we have to make is to abandon the fallacy that, somewhere, somehow, everything is going to turn out all right. We have to be ready to be as foresighted, as determined, as ready to work and to go on working, as are our busy Communist comrades. We must be prepared to match them, policy for policy, vision for vision, ideal for ideal.

I must confess that I can see no inherent reason why such a re-dedication of ourselves to great tasks should be impossible. We have the resources available; we have more resources at our disposal than any group of nations in the history of man. And it is hard to believe that we have run out of the moral energy needed to make the change. Looking at our society I certainly do not feel that it already presents such an image of the good life that we can afford to say that we have contributed all that we can to the vision of a transfigured humanity. Our uncontrollably sprawling cities, our shapeless suburbia, our trivial pursuits—quiz shows, TV, the golf games—hardly add up to the final end of man. We can do better than this. We also have the means to do better. If we do not feel the need there is only one explanation. We no longer have the vital imagination for the task.

Let us suppose, however, that we slough off our innate complacency. What ought we to try to do? What should be our aim in the challenging testing-period that lies ahead when the aspirations of the poor nations are going to become more and more urgent? For let us have no doubt about this. So far we have been living through the more comfortable phase of transformation in the under-developed areas; we have seen them during a time when their concentrated effort to get rid of colonialism gave them political unity and a sense of national purpose which they may well lack now that independence is achieved. Now that they are running their own affairs, all the grim problems of life face them in the raw: their bounding birth-rates, their lack of capital, their desperate poverty, and, above all, the rising expectations of their own people. Every leader who has led his nation to the overthrow of Western influence or colonial rule is now faced with the stark problem: 'What next?' Whether he is a Nasser in Egypt, a Kasim in Iraq, an Azikiwe in Nigeria, a Nkrumah in Ghana, or even —in a more hopeful setting—a Nehru in India, he still must answer the question. There are no evasions now, no blaming it on the West—though that temptation continues—no looking for outside scapegoats. So, by a paradox, the post-colonial period is more tense, dangerous, and uncertain than the colonial struggle itself.

What can we do? What sort of policies can help the developing nations in the crucial years that lie ahead? And if I give you something of a shorthand answer, it is because we have already discussed a number of the crucial changes that must be made. Let us be clear first of all over the general aim. During the next twenty to thirty years we hope to see a majority of the developing nations pass through the sound-barrier of sustained growth. Moreover, we want these societies to have political elbow-room with a measure of autonomy for different groups and political power organized on a plural basis. We do not specify institutions or ideologies; but we hope for open societies in an open world. How shall we set about it?

The first point to make is that some general strategy is needed. And strategy is inseparable from a sustained effort through time. The rhythm of growth is not the rhythm of annual budgets and appropriations. Unless the Western nations bring themselves to accept the need for five- and ten-year programs, they will even waste what they do spend, for it will not be geared into a genuine strategy of growth.

The next point is that the scale of aid must be adequate. Patchy development, a little here, a little there, does not lead to sustained growth. In every developing economy, there comes a time when, for perhaps two decades, a 'big push' is needed to get the economy off the launching-pad and into orbit.

Not all nations come to that point at the same time. There seems to be a certain pattern of progress and expansion, and different economies are ranged at different points along the line. First there is a phase that one might call the 'pre-investment' phase. Nearly everything needed for a 'big push' in investment is still lacking. Educated people are not available, training is minimal, capital overheads or infra-structure—power, transport, harbours, housing—have still to be built. At this stage, the country must be prepared for a later plunge into investment and help with education and training, investment in infra-structure, surveys of resources, and some preliminary planning, are the great needs.

But at the next stage—where such countries as India or Brazil or Mexico now stand—the big investments begin to pay off. The ground is laid, rapid growth can be secured. It is at this point that large-scale capital aid from abroad can offset local poverty and lack of capital, thereby sparing governments the cruel choice of using totalitarian methods to compel people to save. Of all the countries at this stage of growth, I would say that India is the most important. The framework of a functioning economy is already built. But its ambitious capital plans are gravely endangered by a critical shortage of foreign exchange. In any Western development-strategy for the next decade, I myself would hope to see something like a billion dollars a year reserved for India's foreign exchange bill. If India can achieve its break-through, it is not only a question of India's preparedness. Nearly half the people living in the under-developed areas will be on their way to the modern world. If one adds Pakistan, more than half the problem of under-development could be met there in the Indian sub-continent.

Given that we accept the philosophy of a 'big push' in aid and investment, once the pre-conditions of growth have been realized, where should the capital be directed? It is quite impossible to define a general strategy since each country varies so much in its capacities, in its endowment of resources, in the scale of its internal market, and its export prospects. But perhaps one or two general points are worth making here. The first is that investment in education must continue to receive strong emphasis. Recent studies suggest that between sixty and fifty per cent of the gains in productivity made in the West in the last half-century spring from better trained minds, from more research, and more systematic use of the economy's brain-power. At present, most of the developing economies are only in the very first stages of the needed advance in education. Africa is strewn with societies where not more than ten per cent of the people are literate, where perhaps only one per cent ever reach secondary levels of schooling. The final tragic consequence of these standards can be seen in the Congo which became independent with perhaps not more than a dozen people with university degrees. No modern economy can be built on this basis.

A second critical area is that of farming. Modernized

agriculture is, as we have seen, indispensable to the creation of general momentum in the economy. There are two separate needs: to encourage the structural changes which modern agriculture demands—the land reforms, the consolidation of holdings, the building of an influential co-operative movement; and to ensure a sufficient flow of capital into farming. The great variety of modern techniques, new fertilizers, new seed, new methods in planting and tilling, are nearly all costly. So is the scale of credit needed to launch a successful co-operative system. So last of all are the agricultural extension systems without which the farmer cannot learn what new opportunities are open to him. In the past, agriculture has been all too often the last on the government's priority list. Modern experience suggests it should be moved to the top.

The third area of expansion—industry—shows such universal variety that most generalizations have little value. However, one or two comments have some validity. One can say that industrialization will proceed more rapidly if a mistaken sense of national prestige does not precipitate large and costly mistakes in planning, such as investing in an integrated steel-works where there is neither iron ore nor coking-coal. Programs will lead to a better use of resources if capital is recognized for what it is in all developing economies: extremely scarce. Its price should be high, even if this idea upsets the more usual concept that basic services should be kept cheap in order to stimulate growth.

Another aspect of the same problem is that since

foreign exchange is the scarcest of all forms of capital, it may be necessary, by high import duties or by auctioning import licences, or by other measures, to ensure that the entrepreneur who gets his hands on foreign exchange pays for its full value. This approach may contradict another tendency—to overvalue a developing nation's currency so that its exports will buy a maximum amount of foreign supplies. But, then, the way to development is, as Professor Benjamin Higgins once remarked, 'paved with vicious circles.'

A developing government should aim its policies at ensuring the quickest rate of capital accumulation. Profits should be strongly encouraged, in public as in private enterprise, and tax-systems arranged so that all the incentives are towards their reinvestment. This again does not always arouse much enthusiasm among planners brought up to believe in the inherent immorality of profits and ready to run essential public services on a 'no profit, no loss' basis. But profits are one of the chief means by which resources can be put at the disposal of the investors in society and, as we have seen, are a major source of investment in Soviet Russia.

When it comes to the actual content of industrial policy, it must fit local conditions. Most countries can begin to produce locally some of the goods they import, provided protection is given. The 'beer, boots, and bricks' stage of consumer industry only awaits a determined government and some local entrepreneurial talent. But large-scale industry depends upon the availability of crucial raw materials. And it depends, too, upon the scale of the internal market. Five large steel-plants in India, where over four hundred million people make up the market and where iron ore and coking-coal are available, make perfect sense. East Europe's proliferation of steel-mills after 1948 did not. Clearly, developing governments would be well advised to look round and see whether by customs unions or common markets with their neighbours they may not increase the size and efficiency of their industrial units without risk of over-production.

To all these changes—in education, in farming, in industry—there are more than economic consequences. Investment in men, investment in new techniques, investment in new forms of activity, all widen and strengthen the managerial and professional class and increase the training and scope of the manual worker. That gradual extension of the middle class to cover more and more of the nation's citizens is set in motion. With it goes a brighter hope of rational politics and civil rights.

These, then, are some of the elements in a broad strategy of modernization. But I think we have to realize that we in the Western world are not now organized to accomplish anything of the kind. It may be true that for nearly a hundred years we have been a kind of inter-connected economy, taking some seventy per cent of each other's foreign investment, engrossing nearly seventy per cent of world trade, and affecting each other radically by the shifts and changes in our economic policy. But here Mr. Micawber has reigned; here, above

(148)

all, we have assumed that if everybody pursues his own national interest to the limit, the outcome will somehow be to the advantage of everybody else. But this is very far from being generally true. Everyone's decision in 1929—as the recession deepened—to cut imports and push exports reduced world trade by three-quarters in nine months. The recession itself had been in some measure sparked by the fact that between 1925 and 1929 Britain did not dare reflate its economy for fear of losing its foreign reserves and America dared not deflate its wild boom for fear of attracting even more of the world's gold. Now if we think that this unreconciled opposite pull between domestic and foreign interest is a thing of the past, let us remember that all though 1960 we saw comparable pressures between the German mark and the dollar. In short, we have not yet worked out the policies and institutions needed to overcome the conflicting interests in our interdependent Atlantic world. In fact, only once did we have such a policy: during the Marshall Plan when for a time, owing to America's generosity and leadership, the nations of the Atlantic area walked in step towards common goals.

Today, I believe we have to revive the Marshall spirit if we are to have any hope of dealing—and dealing in time—with the problem of our obligations to the underdeveloped areas. Once again, I can suggest only in shorthand terms some of the policies we should undertake if we were a genuine community of rich nations dedicated to the task of creating the prosperity and the well-being of the developing world. And perhaps I should add, in parenthesis, that in doing so we should expand our own well-being as well. To me, one of the most vivid proofs that there is a moral governance in the universe is the fact that when men or governments work intelligently and far-sightedly for the good of others, they achieve their own prosperity too. Take our Western experience with the welfare state. We did not plan to do it as a good stroke of business. It was a moral decision with ancient antecedents. Yet one of the consequences has been to reduce business risks. Mass consumption, secured by social security, enables the economy to avoid the booms and collapses of the old economy.

I believe we should see the same outcome if in the world economy we could determine to build up the purchasing power of the poorer nations. We should find that, once again, our own prosperity had been helped by the underpinning of world consumption and by the creation of a world economy free from the ups and downs, the uncertainties and incoherences, of the system as we know it today.

'Honesty is the best policy' used to be said in Victorian times. I would go further. I would say that generosity is the best policy and that expansion of opportunity sought for the sake of others ends by bringing well-being and expansion to oneself. The dice are not hopelessly loaded against us. Our morals and our interests—seen in true perspective—do not pull apart. Only the narrowness of our own interests, whether personal or national, blinds us to this moral truth.

What then should we do? Our first step must be a commitment. All the wealthy nations must accept a common obligation to provide capital and technical assistance to the under-developed areas. Britain, Canada, Australia, Western Europe: we must all begin to do our share. Let us be quite clear about one thing. The reason why there is trouble over the American balance of payments is nothing to do with the inherent strength of the American economy, which is vast. It is nothing to do with the American trade balance, which is favourable. It has something to do, admittedly, with the American export of capital. But, above all, it is created by the fact that America is carrying far more than its fair burden both of the defence of the free world and of aid to the developing nations. And before we can hope to have a functioning Atlantic economy the other member nations must play their part. A suggested one per cent of national income is a fair criterion; and, incidentally, I consider that Germany, so generously rebuilt after the war and so generously forgiven the enormous destruction which Hitler created, might be in the forefront of those who accept this obligation.

This commitment is, however, only the beginning of the matter. Such a common purpose needs the proper institutional form. I believe we should attempt to build up in our Atlantic world some of the institutions which make it possible for us to co-operate *within* the national community. I think we should have an Atlantic Reserve Bank. I think we should develop common strategies for development and investment both inside and outside the Atlantic arena. I think we should take a long, hard look at our trade policies, particularly the prices we pay for primary products. At present they do not, as they once did, pull up the rest of the world behind us. On the contrary, they tend to widen the gap. And for all this I think we need to expand our present Atlantic Organization for Economic Development into as many institutions—banks, development funds, trade groups, common markets, statistical services, and, above all, common policy-making organs—which might be needed to knit our interdependent economy into an integrated whole.

If we did this, I think we should do more than simply provide ourselves with the means to work out a strategy for the developing world; we should be creating the economic pre-conditions of a functioning world order. After all, we know that inside our domestic society we cannot survive in peace without law and welfare. It is upon these two pivots that the health of a community depends. Is our narrow interdependent world so different? Should we not be trying to create in the world at large the basic pre-conditions of a peaceful society?

We recognize the principles more or less inside our own domestic community. We do not have private wars. The rich do indeed contribute to the advancement of the poor. And while I am not concerned here with the whole great issue of world law and of disarmament, I am deeply concerned with the second aspect of good order: the ability of the rich to recognize their obligations and to see that in an interdependent world

—and Heaven knows our interdependence cannot be denied when we all stand under the shadow of atomic destruction—the principles of the general welfare cannot stop at the limits of our frontiers. It has to go forward; it has to include the whole family of man.

And having said so much, I begin to wonder whether there are any forces inside our comfortable, cosy, complacent Western world that will make us accept this challenge and see that we now face thirty to forty years of world-building on a scale never known in human history, since all our forefathers lived without the community of science, the speed of transport, the whole interconnectedness of the modern globe. What will spur us to face this kind of decision? Facts? The facts are there. We cannot wish away the great revolution of modernization that is sweeping round the world; we cannot say it would be easier or more pleasant if it had not happened. Perhaps so; but we started the revolution and we can hardly ignore the forces that we unleashed upon the world.

Should we be guided by fear? Fear can indeed be the beginning of wisdom. Those who can live comfortably and without perturbation under the hideous threat of atomic destruction do not seem to me to be very wise. But blind fear is not a constructive force. Fear will serve us only if it drives us on to find a way out of our fears. And there is only one: to leave behind our present community of potential annihilation and build a community of moral purpose in its place. In such a world public law would take the place of private violence and the general welfare would be accepted over and above the particular interests of particular communities; above all, mankind would discover, beneath the clash of ideology, some minimum standards of trust rooted in the fact that we are all men, that we all stand under the judgment of history, and that we all love and seek to live and know that we must die.

It is just because the task before us is the positive task of building a peaceful home for the human family that I doubt whether realism or fear is enough to set us to work. We need resources of faith and vision as well. Do we have them? Or have the revolutions of our day, while increasing our physical powers, damped down the ardours of our spirit?

I do not believe it. Every one of the revolutions we have discussed goes beyond our material concerns and offers a challenge to the quality of our mind and spirit. The equality of men which is such a driving force all round the world sprang originally from the Western sense that men, as souls of infinite metaphysical value, stand equal before the throne of God. And if we feel this equality of man as a profound, moral fact, can we really be content to see men hungry, to see men die, to see men continue in starvation and ill-health when we have the means to help them? Is this our concept of equality? If it is, do we not betray our faith?

Then, again, our concern with worldly things is not mere materialism. It has in it an essential element of religious insight. God looked on his universe and found it good. The materials offered us in farm and factory can be set to work to create a community in which no one need starve or go naked and unhoused. We can 'redeem the time' by setting matter to work for the greater good of all our brothers, who are all mankind. The Christian God who bade His followers feed the hungry and heal the sick and took His parables from the homely round of daily work gave material things His benediction. It has not faded because material things are more abundant now.

Science itself—this vision of an orderly world in which matter does not respond to chaotic promptings but to some vast harmony of universal law—is in no way incompatible with a vision of moral order in which it can be the tool of a better life for all mankind. Science has removed us from the heaviest bondage of the past: the fact that material resources were always too scarce to match even the greatest goodwill. Only a hundred years ago, if we had wished to give covering, food, shelter, and a simple education to the mass of mankind, we could not have done so because our material means were not equal to the task. What science has done has been to set us free. It has delivered us from the bondage of our material poverty and opened a great area of choice where vision and will can operate because they have the physical means at hand.

Science, understood in this sense, is indeed a means of liberty. Perhaps you have wondered why I have not mentioned freedom as the greatest revolution of our time. Quite frankly, the reason is that I am not sure whether it *is* one of the spreading revolutions of this

Freedom

century. There are times when I feel that, in our Western world, freedom rather resembles the Biblical talent that was put in a napkin and buried in the ground. We have it—but do we use it? On the issue of freedom, the revolutions of our day are all ambiguous. The revolution of equality does not necessarily imply freedom. All prisoners in a jail are equal. But they are not free. The revolution of science offers the means of freedom. But it can be used as well for making dictatorship more efficient and war more dire. And materialism, misunderstood as a false overconcern with the things of this world, a false worship of 'the idols of the market place and the idols of the tribe,' can create the reverse of true freedom if men and women become more and more entangled in their own clamant and unassuageable wants. Our revolutions will not do our work for us. They can yield us freedom or its opposite. The outcome depends on us, and I sometimes wonder whether we have made any very fundamental attempt to interpret the revolutions of our time in the light of freedom. Have we measured the margin of choice given us by our new capital resources, our new technology, our new ability to create the means of wealth? Have we understood that this liberty of action must be used? It cannot, it must not be left to rust with us. And given our ability to assist in the process of modernization, have we really grasped its relevance to the grand question of our time: whether the developing world society will be closed or open, slave or free?

After all, constitutional liberty is a sophisticated concept. Between Magna Charta and our present-day democracy there lie eight hundred years of experience and feeling our way. I am not a determinist. I do not believe that economic forces necessarily create political forms. On the contrary, I believe freedom to have been one of the innate formative ideas of our Western way of life. But equally I observe that its incorporation in concrete institutions did presuppose some economic and social changes. The emergence of a strong middle class after the Middle Ages helped to secure rights and liberties to a larger and larger group of articulate and responsible citizens. In the nineteenth century, the growth of wealth and the spread of literacy encouraged the extension of democratic privileges even further, and complete adult suffrage and complete adult literacy arrived at about the same time.

I think it is probably a safe assumption that something of the same pattern must be expected in emergent societies; though they need not wait so long since models of change already exist. A strong expanding professional and managerial class, a strong thrust of literacy, and the expanding resources both presuppose are almost certainly pre-conditions of political development in freedom. We are, I think, irrational when we suddenly expect those who emerge from primitive societies to seize our concepts of liberty intact, forgetting the long intervening history of our own experiments. If we are not to be disappointed, I think we must seek with new energy and commitment to fill in the historical gap. We need to be far more active in the

way of economic aid, capital investment, and educational assistance. We need to work with far more purpose to create the framework of general literacy and
personal responsibility. We need to be far more imaginative in showing that we regard the right of nations
to govern themselves as only the first, essential, but
preliminary, step in creating the conditions in which
nations can be truly free. But the next step is equally
vital: to give concrete substance to the experience of
national liberty and not permit it to become a time of
lessening opportunity and hope.

But I have the impression that when we talk so con-
fidently of liberty, we are unaware of the awful servi-
tudes that are created by the ancient enemies of mankind: the servitude of poverty when means are so small
that there is literally no choice at all; the servitude of
ignorance when there are no perspectives to which the
mind can open because there is no education on which
the mind can begin to work; the servitude of ill-health
which means that the expectation of life is almost too
short to allow for any experience of freedom, and the
years that *are* lived are dragged out without the health
and strength which are themselves a liberation.

Because we have interpreted freedom in too narrow
a sense and assumed that people will find the outer
form of freedom natural when none of its actual substantial content has been realized, there has been something empty about our advocacy of the free way of life.
What is the free way of life to a tribal society which does
not know whether it can eat next week? What is the

free way of life to an ancient society where illiteracy bars most people from any of the benefits of freedom? What, above all, can freedom be said to mean when the nations who talk of it most incessantly seem to have so little awareness of its wider moral dimensions? Am I free if my brother is bound by hopeless poverty and ignorance? Am I a prophet of the free way of life if I reveal perfect indifference to the plight of the man who has 'fallen among thieves,' the man whom the good Samaritan helped while the others passed him by?

If we want to spread the revolution of liberty round the world to complete and reconcile the other great revolutions of our day, we have to re-examine its moral content and ask ourselves whether we are not leaving liberty as a wasted talent and allowing other forces, not friendly to liberty, to monopolize the great vision of men working in brotherhood to create a world in which all can live. But God is not mocked. We reap what we sow and if freedom for us is no more than the right to pursue our own self-interest—personal or national—then we can make no claim to the greatest vision of our society: 'the glorious liberty of the sons of God.' Without vision we, like other peoples, will perish. But if it is restored, it can be as it always has been the profoundest inspiration of our society, and can give our way of life its continuing strength.